THE LOST DISCIPLINE
OF CONVERSATION

ALSO BY JOANNE J. JUNG

Character Formation in
Online Education

Knowing Grace: Cultivating
a Lifestyle of Godliness

Godly Conversation: Rediscovering
the Puritan Practice of Conference

THE
LOST DISCIPLINE OF
CONVERSATION

SURPRISING LESSONS
*in Spiritual Formation Drawn from
the English Puritans*

JOANNE J. JUNG

ZONDERVAN

The Lost Discipline of Conversation
Copyright © 2018 by Joanne J. Jung

ISBN 978-0-310-53897-4 (ebook)

Requests for information should be addressed to:
Zondervan, *3900 Sparks Dr. SE, Grand Rapids, Michigan 49546*

Library of Congress Cataloging-in-Publication Data

Names: Jung, Joanne J., author.
Title: The lost discipline of conversation : surprising lessons in spiritual formation drawn
    from the English Puritans / Joanne J. Jung.
Description: Grand Rapids, Michigan : Zondervan, [2018] | Includes bibliographical
    references.
Identifiers: LCCN 2018018504| ISBN 9780310538967 (pbk.) | ISBN 9780310538974
    (e-book)
Subjects: LCSH: Conversation--Religious aspects--Christianity. | Listening--Religious
    aspects--Christianity. | Spiritual formation--Puritans.
Classification: LCC BV4597.53.C64 J86 2018 | DDC 241/.672--dc23 LC record
    available at https://lccn.loc.gov/2018018504

Cover Illustration by Gary W. Alexander
Art direction: Tammy Johnson
Interior design: Denise Froehlich

Printed in the United States of America

18 19 20 21 22 /DHV/ 10 9 8 7 6 5 4 3 2 1

So to Him who is worthy of all worship and praise, thank You. I remain humbled and amazed at the countless ways You have guided, surprised, encouraged, and provided words, ideas, templates, resources, friends, and family. Thank You, and for You, this work of my heart and hands, Your Majesty.

CONTENTS

Foreword by Kyle Strobel................................... 11

A Word from the Author................................. 13

Acknowledgments...................................... 15

Introduction... 17

PART I—REDISCOVERING A "LOST" MEANS OF GRACE

1. Our Viral Hunger for Sacred Community............... 23

2. What the Means of Grace Mean....................... 29

3. The Word Heard, Read, and Remembered.............. 35

4. "A Kind of Paradise": When Souls Were Refreshed 45

5. Peek to Pique: Features of Conference 53

PART II—CONFERENCE IN VARIOUS LIFE CONTEXTS

6. Small (and Deeper) Group Conferences 67

7. Family Conferences of the Conversation Kind........... 83

8. Marriage Conferences of the Conversation Kind........ 103

9. From Pastor to Pew and Back Again. 117

10. Not Your Typical Pastors Conference. 129

11. Distance Conferencing: From Signed Letters
     to Streaming Sunday Services 143

PART III—SOUL-TO-SOUL BIBLE STUDIES:
CONFERENCING THROUGH GOD'S WORD 159

Matthew 1:1–16 162

Matthew 12:29–32; Matthew 13:22–32 167

Matthew 13:1–23 169

John 15:1–12. 172

Philippians 4:1–3 178

Colossians 3:1–17 183

Hebrews 12:1–3 188

Appendices. 194

Notes 215

FOREWORD

When I first started studying Puritan spirituality, I could not believe the riches I found. I felt as if I needed to glance over my shoulder, as if I'd uncovered a secret treasure that someone purposefully hid from view. Like many of those raised in evangelicalism, I came to believe I had to go outside of my own tradition to find real spiritual depth. I discovered in time that nothing is further from the truth. Richard Lovelace, in his work *Dynamics of Spiritual Life*, coined the term "The Sanctification Gap" and addresses our failure to attend to the abundance in our own spiritual tradition. He claims, "There seemed to be a sanctification gap among Evangelicals, a peculiar conspiracy somehow to mislay the Protestant tradition of spiritual growth and concentrate on frantic witnessing activity, sermons on John 3:16 and theological arguments over eschatological subtleties."[1] While evangelicalism is no longer mired in "eschatological subtleties," Lovelace's critique remains as accurate now as it was nearly four decades ago. There is a sanctification gap in the evangelical church—we recognize the difficulties of the Christian life, but we do not know where to find the answers.

It was not until I started working on *Formed for the Glory of God: Learning from the Spiritual Practices of Jonathan Edwards* that I began to pull together a synthesis of Puritan spirituality. Once again I was confronted with a treasure that had remained lost, the very treasure Lovelace names. I discovered depth of insight concerning things like meditation, church practice, and prayer, but what caught my attention most was a spiritual practice called "conferencing." The problem with exposing Edwards's view of conferencing was that he rarely talked *about* it, but instead would drop the term into letters or sermons as a practice he supposed was obvious. Edwards did not talk *about* conferencing because he had read his Puritan heritage deeply and simply accepted their insights. His role as a pastor was not to introduce his people to conferencing, they knew what it was, but to encourage, teach, and shepherd his people in the practice through his sermons, pastoral care, and his own personal practice. In other words, what Edwards was able to assume—that everyone knows and understands conferencing—is something we cannot assume at all. There is a sanctification gap in evangelicalism, and we need to recover the wisdom of our fathers and mothers in the faith.

What Joanne Jung has done in this book is recognize a key aspect of this sanctification gap and address it in a way few of us could. Instead of simply prodding readers to pick up Puritan works, Joanne walks us into their insights directly, shepherding us through their wisdom and showing how we can recover it for the church today. The goal is not simply understanding our tradition, but learning from it so that we can follow Christ more profoundly. In particular, conference guides us into meaningful, authentic, and life-changing relationships, providing a map for how we can give ourselves to a deeper sort of existence. In an age of social media, where people are trained to relate *at* one another and not *with* them, conferencing provides a desperately needed remedy to our spiritual amnesia. Read this book, but do not merely read it, follow its directions into a way of being with your brothers and sisters in Christ.

KYLE STROBEL

A Word from the Author

If you are at all familiar with the works of the English Puritans, then you'll understand why I chuckled when we decided on this title, *The Lost Discipline of Conversation: Surprising Lessons in Spiritual Formation Drawn from the English Puritans*. It's a little long but would have been considered brief in the Puritans' minds. For instance, here is the actual title of John Bunyan's *Pilgrim's Progress*: *The Pilgrim's Progress from this world to that which is to come, delivered under the similitude of a dream, shewing the several difficulties and dangers he met with, and the many victories he obtained over the world, the flesh, and the Devil, together with his happy arrival at the Celestial City, and the glory and joy he found to his eternal comfort.* Their titles clearly described the contents of their works. No guessing was needed. If you're not familiar with Puritan works, then welcome! I was a stranger to them just fifteen years ago, and since then they have become some of my best old dead friends. Under great and unthinkable persecution, they took to their pens. From that treasury we have the preserved works of practical theologians, physicians of the soul, and passionate thinkers. Men and women contributed to their own and others' spiritual growth, and one key way was through conversation.

Step into their world and then step out into yours, having been impacted by the richness and depth of their Christ-centeredness and others-focus.

ACKNOWLEDGMENTS

For the support and love of Norm, Adriane and Sean, Ashley, Cami and Tyler, and Mason and Miles, I am indebted. My deans and chair at Talbot School of Theology, Clint Arnold, Scott Rae, Doug Huffman, and Matt Williams, granted a research leave to complete this book. Many encouraged me with their prayers, sent notes, and offered time and space to research, think, reflect, and write. Others reviewed, gave feedback, edited, laughed, asked questions, and painted—giving your part to this book and to me. Thank you.

My colleague Ken Berding and I reflected on his desire for scholarship to be worshipful. I desire the same.

INTRODUCTION

I was recently asked, "What is it like to be still before God, to be in His presence?" After some time pondering with and before God, I penned my observations.

When a human being is relaxed, observe the hands. They do not lie flat. Instead, they are cupped, as if in a natural posture to receive. But cupped hands face downward. In order to receive, they have to be positioned accordingly. Beggars know to hold their cups right side up. In the same way, being in God's presence is relaxed and still, yet with the intentional posture of receiving. Receive His words, not of condemnation or criticism but of welcome. Receive His touch, not a slap, hit, or strike but an accepting embrace. Receive the sense of His intimate power, not of violence or attack but of protection and wisdom. Receive the dewdrops of refreshing, deeper, longer, and unlabored breaths; the persuading silence of His outstretched arms; and the settling posture of His welcoming you. No pretense. No spin. No image-managing. All my thoughts, words, and sighs are directed to Him. Oftentimes, it seems He is the only one who really wants them.

By extension, this can be experienced in community. We can, in conversation, be as Christ to one another, or to another. God desires that our conversations reflect and ultimately direct us and others to Him. Yet there is a lot working against us.

The growing epidemic of social isolation is killing us. "A great paradox of our hyper-connected digital age is that we seem to be drifting apart," wrote Dhruv Khullar, a resident physician at Massachusetts General Hospital, in an editorial to the *New York Times*. We have many acquaintances but not many friends. "Increasingly, however, research confirms our deepest intuition: Human connection lies at the heart of human well-being."[1] Unfortunately, we have grown accustomed to distance in our relationships.

When engaged in conversations, we sometimes answer for others or inadequately for ourselves, as when the well-meaning restaurant server asks, "Is everything good?" and we are mid-sentence, mid-thought, or with a mouth full. We offer a thumbs up or a nod of agreement. Asking questions that answer themselves does not allow much room for two-way conversations. Perhaps many of us have become trained in this way so as to limit the possibility of time-consuming dialogue. When such an approach is translated into everyday discussions, they become short-circuited. Our self-affirming, "This is a great idea, right?" or the addition of, "You know what I mean?" are met with a thumbs up or a nod of agreement.

Often in our conversations, we take polite turns, flipping back and forth between partners. Researchers have found that the typical gap between turns is 200 milliseconds,[2] and this is true across cultures and even in sign language.[3] Formulation of words for a genuine dialogue requires more time. Thus partners in conversations will predict or assume the rest of a sentence and build responses during our partner's turn. Equipped with our "hypothetical rejoinders," conversation partners quickly seize the next available opportunity to speak.

These observations are striking when applied to our conversations of spiritual matters. If these conversations even take place, they are often not conducive to going into the depths that would foster Christlike transformation.

For optimal spiritual health, conversations on spiritual matters matter. They speak into our desire to know and be known by God and one another and to do so in community. We thrive on this type of community; our present reality reflects a viral hunger and need for it. Over the centuries, our conversations have suffered a decline in meaningful dialogue, intentional engagement, and selfless attentive listening, especially in matters of a spiritual nature. We have settled for quick exchanges when the selfless presence, attentive listening, and thought-filled words of a sustained conversation would better meet the needs of the soul. We are in need of a recovery.

As we travel through the archives of history, a recovery can be found in the pages of four-hundred-year-old treatises, sermons, diaries, and letters. The English Puritans of the sixteenth and seventeenth centuries exercised a practice that stands in stark contrast to our forgettable, superficial, and all-too-brief conversations. The observer discovers a forgotten treasure, the common spiritual practice of "conference." The root word "confer" can mean "the action of bringing together," and "to talk together on an important subject"[4] and was once described in the seventeenth century as involving "the freedom of speaking and conferring the thoughts of the heart."[5] Characterized by a heightened ability to be present before God and others, these reflective conversations of the Puritans were particularly meaningful and transformative for participants of a sacred community. We learn this from these saints of the past: Be a gift. Be present.

PART I

REDISCOVERING A "LOST" MEANS OF GRACE

CHAPTER 1

OUR VIRAL HUNGER FOR SACRED COMMUNITY

I wish you more we than me.

> Amy Krouse Rosenthal and Tom
> Lichtenheld, *I Wish You More*

Excavators continue to extract Terra Cotta warriors from the site in Xian, China. In the third century BC, an emperor created thousands of the life-size ceramic soldiers, with no two alike. Together with attending horses and chariots, they were expected to accompany the emperor into the hereafter, wherever he would reside and rule. Reflecting on the years of detailed craftsmanship, labor, and effort required for the creation of each of the collection's figures baffles the mind, suggesting even this thirteen-year-old boy emperor knew something of eternity and community.

Nearly 2,500 years later, people still sense something about community; it remains a longing because for many it represents an unmet yearning. Maybe you have discovered that putting a few people together in a room and calling it a small group does not automatically mean you have community; having a militia of clay soldiers does not an army make. Having monthly, biweekly, or even weekly meetings does not necessarily translate to deep, meaningful relationships that further one's growth in the Christian life.

The fragmentation that characterizes our society persists. It is a sad but accurate appraisal that in our contemporary society we are held captive by Netflix, Facebook, the internet, television, and Amazon. We are victims of a repertoire of fast-food menus, instant gratification, and overcrowded, conflicting, and unrelenting schedules. Our entertainment-soaked culture, which wrestles with boredom, thrills, and materialism, has contributed to the sensory overload common to urban life. Our addiction to information technology with its online connections, news and internet communication, websites, blogs, and streaming (to name a few) exacerbates the preexisting flood of intruding must-haves and must-dos that demand our time, attention, affections, and devotion.

External factors such as mobility—people moving out of town, out of state, out of sight, and hence, out of mind—have taken their toll on community. To complicate matters, researchers say that our circle of friends—with whom we are most comfortably honest and vulnerable—is shrinking. The number has decreased over the past ten years, and it shows no signs of a change in course.[1] Many people are completely isolated from those with whom important matters could be discussed.[2] These same researchers, over a decade earlier, found that those with whom we have close and strong ties influence us and indirectly shape the kinds of people we become.[3]

Couple this with internal factors that contribute to the demise of face-to-face sharing of life. Consider the isolationism and pervasive individualism that has permeated our culture and it is no wonder why authentic spiritual transformation fostered in community is threatened. Our society is often described as being composed of individualists who are taught from early childhood to be independent. We are warned not to let anyone get too close. Any disclosure of hurts, doubts, or weaknesses should be reserved for a select few, if any at all. A perceived lack of strength or determination would reflect a flaw in character and render one unhealthy or unable to live out a full and meaningful life. We are convinced that anything worth doing is best done by oneself. One expects to "go it alone." This thinking infiltrates our approach to others in our small groups, as Dallas Willard has described fellowship as often no more than "well-calculated distance."[4] However, if our spiritual and emotional hurts were as visible as an open wound or a gash on our leg or arm, we would have to seek help and allow others to help as well.

These few comments, collected from friends and acquaintances about their involvement in small groups, reveal not only fears and disappointments but a desire for greater substance and deeper engagement.

- "There are really nice people in my small group, but I don't think they'd like me if they really knew me. I feel inadequate."
- "Small groups are only for people my age and my husband's age. I wish our pastor would put us in an older group because all I want is wisdom. I don't want to hear other moms complain about their daily routine (life). It's depressing."
- "We spend more time just discussing how our week went, and it becomes a group therapy session."
- "So little time is spent studying God's Word together. And when we do, everyone just gives the 'pat' and safe answers. I walk away thinking I could have done this at home."
- "We spend more time eating and 'fellowshipping' than really getting to know each other."
- "Some of the members dominate the discussions, and those of us who are more introverted have thoughts but contribute little."
- "I've realized I don't know how to relate to people when face-to-face. I'm more unsure of myself. It's uncomfortable, and I'd rather not place myself in that situation."
- "I don't believe I have anything important to contribute."

Relationships take time and effort; these are precious commodities. We end up sharing less with fewer people. The result: unattended souls.

Symptoms of unattended souls are wide and many. Diagnosis is not difficult. Pridefulness and self-centeredness. Bitterness. Loneliness. The tendency to doubt. The tendency to compare. Regrets. Depression. Envy. Anger. Fear. Hopelessness. Guilt. Insecurity. Feeling unlovable. Being short-tempered with the people I love most. Experiencing waves of unworthiness. Feeling fake and empty. Being motivated by peer approval, controlling, defensive. Engaging only in small talk. Feeling inadequate. Mask-wearing. Holding grudges more and longer. Wasting hours on the computer or in front of the TV. Intolerance. Unforgiveness. Apathy.

So how is your soul?

To even mention the word *soul* elicits questions. What is the soul? What does the soul need? In sum, every human being is a soul. It is the whole of who we are, body and spirit, and we are created by God to connect with Him and others. Because God created and designed us as souls, our needs will align with who God is, the Triune community in which He exists, and a healthy Christian community. The human soul thrives on and is nurtured in relationship with God and others. Christians depend on God, His Spirit, His Word, and others for spiritual sustenance, our identity in Christ, and for the very formation of our faith. The decline in attending to the health of souls is becoming evident in the lack of vibrant life and relationships both inside and outside the church.

The small-group movement has sought to address this problem. Small groups undertook serious efforts to contend with the effects of fragmentation and anonymity in society. No matter the degree of "rugged individualism" or self-determination one adopts, the individualist may eventually find herself or himself in some sort of small group in order to address the issues and challenges of life. Yet as Christians, we often overemphasize actions and fail to attend to one another as souls. Many have had "accountability partners." These consist of relationships where friends keep each other in check, making sure the other is doing well and avoiding temptation. This approach alone causes people to scrutinize each other's actions, without addressing the heart-seeded drive behind these behaviors. It is important for Christians to be accountable to each other; however, this approach misses a critical component because we can be our own best actors. What must complement accountability is attentiveness, being attentive to one another's hearts and souls, in relationships that seek to listen, understand, and represent Christ.

Transformation is a process that requires the individual's cooperation and effort, but it is also intended to be accomplished in community with God and others. Spiritual authenticity is the goal, but the context wherein transformation best takes place is critical. The precursor for spiritual authenticity is spiritual receptivity and depth. The kind of community that satisfies the soul is impossible without a revealing relationship with Christ, where He reveals more of Himself and we are enabled to reveal more of ourselves.

We are made in the image of God, an image that is tarnished yet has survived the fall. Who we are is intrinsically connected to who God is. Our spiritual depth, our ability to know ourselves, is linked to knowing God and who He is. This is where God's Word comes into the equation, because the Bible is one of the primary ways God discloses Himself— what He's done, what He's doing, and what He promises to do. Spiritual depth is far more than how well you know the Scriptures; it's knowing the Word of God and the God of the Word, the book and its author. We need a better, more thoughtful understanding of what He is like, what He says, what He expects of those who bear His image and why, and how He empowers those who follow His Son, Jesus.

The convergence of knowledge of God and self that is found in the deepest recesses of your heart shows up in the way you live out what you believe (Proverbs 4:23). The heart, as the control center of the soul, directs our life. Living, then, is the heart in motion. That which enters the heart—what you know, what you feel, where you will to act—affects your attitude and thus your behavior. In Genesis 2:7, God breathes the breath of life into Adam, and he becomes a living soul, a distinct creation of body and spirit. Biblically, the soul is the whole person. Because the soul is both body and spirit, our actions influence our heart as much as our thoughts do.

Spiritual authenticity occurs when faith and experience merge. Our lives are the very places where the truth of what God says in His Word meets us head on in the reality of our moment-by-moment experiences. The more we know and are transformed by truth, the more we discover who we are and find our place in God's history-making plan for humankind.

Human beings are created with the longing for belonging found in community. We were made to experience life with God and with others. Living is best done in community, so to be spiritually influenced is to be spiritually influencing. We long further to live consistently, engaging with others who are like-hearted, together cultivating our vertical relationship with God and our horizontal relationship with others. In community I learn more about who I am and my purpose in life. Who I am is fostered by who I am with. My truest identity is established by God's Word and

Spirit and is cultivated and enriched in the body of Christ, the body in which every part has significance and purpose. Being transparent in this community nurtures open and honest engagement about who we are and who we are becoming through challenges, victories, trials, and the mundane of our lives. Simultaneously, we are motivated by a desire to have a pure heart before God and others, allowing the truth of who God is and how He sees me as my Creator to form the "me in us." This perspective is unique to Christians.

Christians are called to enter and continue in this journey of becoming, becoming who God originally designed us to become, persons of integrity and purpose so that no matter where we are, the time of day, or who we are with, we are the same person of godly character. No pretending. No faking. No spin doctoring. It is the you who is becoming more and more like Christ. This level of integrity requires soul-deep transformation.

Do not wait for someone to ask how you are and then answer with a polite, "Fine." Take a moment to ask yourself, "What is the state of my soul?" Answer as honestly as you can. Share your thoughts with a trusted friend in a soul-to-soul talk. Together, bring your shared impressions and feelings to God. The truest measure of how we are doing is found in the well-being of our souls.

If, as you read the above prompts, a longing was stirred for the kind of community needed for this to happen, a place where these types of conversations can be honored and encouraged, you are among those who recognize the need for community with fellow believers. As the English Puritans will show us, there are a number of contexts where this kind of community and conversation can take place. Their understanding and use of "conference" is found more broadly in their application of the means of grace, or spiritual practices. These were designed to spur transformation, as you will begin to see ahead.

CHAPTER 2

WHAT THE MEANS
OF GRACE MEAN

*Watch your hearts every day. Take notice of the
first declining in grace. Observe yourselves when you
begin to grow dull and listless, and use all means for
quickening. Be much in prayer, meditation, and holy
conference.*

Thomas Watson, *All
Things for Good*, 1663

*I find that the language of "means of grace"
coheres more consistently with the theology of the
Bible about such practices and helps to keep the key
emphases in their proper places.*

David Mathis, *Habits of Grace*

If you have been a Christian for any length of time, you have been
encouraged to exercise spiritual disciplines. These are practices that
help believers become more like Christ. The disciplines are tools or activities we engage in toward that end, and Christians throughout the history
of the church have practiced them. These include, but are not limited to,
regularly reading the Bible, prayer, secluded times of silence and solitude,
and scheduled times to fast. The goal in incorporating these disciplines

for growth and maturity is not to become an expert in a discipline but to evidence a growing knowledge of God, seeing His Spirit manifested in and through us in Christlikeness.

One can determine if this growth in Christlikeness is happening by honestly reflecting and answering two questions based on Matthew 22:37–39 (Deuteronomy 6:5 and Leviticus 19:18): Do I love God more today than I did before? and Do I love people, who matter deeply to God, more today than before? Now, before answering too quickly, consider what Jesus says in John 14:15 and 21. Obedience is an indicator that demonstrates love toward Christ. One's obedience quotient reveals the measure of one's love for Jesus. Being honest, there are times when we must answer no to these questions. No, Lord, I do not love You more today than last year. My obedience is waning. And no, God, I do not love people more today than before. In fact, they have become intrusions in my life or rungs on a ladder to climb toward my self-determined success. An accurate assessment is the first step. The spiritual disciplines are exercised in continuing response to the desire for change, to be more aligned with new creation living (2 Corinthians 5:17).

Spiritual disciplines have been exercised by believers for centuries, but they went by a different name among the English Puritans. Our impressions of the Puritans are often stuck somewhere between the Salem witch trials and *The Scarlet Letter*. It remains challenging to rid our minds of the unrelenting stereotype caricaturing Puritans as grim, killjoy fanatics in black steeple-hats, indifferent to humanity and the splendors of this world. Not only is this branding no longer reasonable, but maintaining this short-sighted view blinds the Christian to a wealth of material that is helpful to Christians today. C. S. Lewis states, "We must picture these Puritans as the very opposite of those who bear that name today: as young, fierce, progressive intellectuals, very fashionable and up-to-date. They were not teetotalers; bishops, not beer, were their special aversion."[1] In Lewis's *Screwtape Letters*, Uncle Screwtape, in seeking to derail a Christian's growth in godliness, remarks proudly to Wormwood upon the distorted reputation created of the Puritans: "All that, your patient would probably classify as 'Puritanism'—and may I remark in passing that the value we have given to that word is one of the really solid triumphs of the last hundred years? By it we rescue annually thousands of humans from temperance, chastity, and sobriety of life."[2]

The Puritans sought to cultivate a biblical worldview by maintaining a high view of Scripture, dependence on the Holy Spirit, and a commitment to developing a holistic, working theology of the spiritual life. This was accomplished by various spiritual disciplines, or "means of grace." These means of grace were understood as unforced rhythms through which God communicated Himself; they were tools graciously extended by God to assist the believer toward conversion and growth in godliness. Describing these rhythms this way helps to keep the key emphasis in its proper place—on God. In response to faith, by and through these means, God would supply the believer with grace sufficient for growth in godly living, or sanctification.

The English Puritans took the Bible, their community, and their growth in godliness seriously. Puritan John Preston says, "For know that the means without God, is but as a pen without Ink, a Pipe without water, or a scabbard without a sword." Preston understood the Spirit's life-giving role for the means of grace and describes the result of engaging these spiritual rhythms: "as water is carried from the wellhead unto the pipe, and so from the pipe unto many places, so the means are as pipes to carry grace into the soul."[3]

|||||||||||||||||||||||||||||||||||||||

HISTORICAL SNAPSHOT

John Preston (1587–1628) was a valued politician, influential teacher, preacher, theologian, and author. His preaching became grounds to call him a "hotter sort of Protestant" and the leading Puritan of the 1620s. Preston's works focus on matters of spirituality and practical godliness as exemplified in his *Saints' Spirituall Strength.*

It was clear to the Puritan divines that in order to live the Christian life—beginning with the preconversion experience, then growing in spiritual maturity while having an impact on one's community—the means were essential. The saint was to guard against depending on the means without God, and on God without the means. Careless and unconscious employment of them yielded shallow souls, "Dwarfs in grace and holiness."[4]

Thomas Watson, a Puritan pastor, understood this. He encouraged an honest observation and assessment of one's life and heart and advised engaging in the means.

||||||||||||||||||||||||||||||||||||

HISTORICAL SNAPSHOT

Thomas Watson (died 1686) was a Puritan writer and pastor in London, known for his effective preaching and public prayer. In *All Things Good*, a study of Romans 8:28, he pens that "showers of affliction water the withering root of their grace and make it flourish more." Watson explains how to use the various means of grace in *Heaven Taken by Storm*.

Watch your hearts every day. Take notice of the first declining in grace. Observe yourselves when you begin to grow dull and listless, and use all means for quickening. Be much in prayer, meditation, and *holy conference*. When the fire is going out you throw on fuel; so when the flame of your love is going out, make use of ordinances and gospel promises, as fuel to keep the fire of your love burning.[5] (italics added)

Conference was a common practice of the English Puritans, as common as prayer and meditation.

If it was not difficult enough to correct our lenses to see the benefit Puritans add to our spiritual formation, we need also to augment our present-day usage of this word "conference." There are conference rooms and calls as well as video, leadership, and regional basketball conferences, yet as a means of grace, conference helped people to grow in authentic community. It will not be found on any contemporary list of spiritual disciplines, but it is found on some lists that are almost four-and-a-half centuries old. Pastors of Old England encouraged their congregations to grow in godliness and set out to help them to this end. A number of treatises written by Puritan ministers, or divines, include exhortations to their congregants to pray, meditate, be watchful, and to exercise conference.

Based on Malachi 3:16, the Puritans understood that God was intimately aware of their conversations and regarded their words with deep interest. So they took conversations, especially spiritual ones, seriously. This was, in part, the biblical support for conference. What would it be like if we knew God cared that much about our conversations and if we took conference seriously? It just might help close the gap between what we know and what we do.

The means of grace are God-bestowing, Christ-affirming, Spirit-sustaining practices we embrace, both individually and corporately, for the purpose of experiencing and expressing growth in godliness.

Soul-deep impact and spiritual transformation via these means are God-ordained objectives. Conference was a familiar and widely practiced means of grace. This practice suited the Puritans as it was rooted in Scripture and its benefits were many and far-reaching. Benefits await us as we rediscover conference for today.

CHAPTER 3

THE WORD HEARD, READ, AND REMEMBERED

It [Scripture] is called a lantern, to direct us, Psalm 119:105; a medicine, to heal us; a guide, to conduct us; a bit, to restrain us; a sword, to defend us; water, to wash us; fire, to inflame us; salt, to season us; milk, to nourish us; wine, to rejoice us; rain, to refresh us; a treasure, to enrich us; and the key, to unlock heaven gates unto us.[1]

Henry Smith, "Food for
New-born babes"

To understand the thoughts and words that fuel and sustain conference is to first grasp a high view of Scripture, pastors, and sermons. Our model, the Puritans, depended on the knowledge from these sources for growth in godliness.

They revered the Bible as "the book of books,"[2] the living Word of the living God. Its authority as the supreme source for knowing God and His will for the church and everyday life make it imperative to digest these words daily. Salvation and growth in godliness are impossible without it. Reverence for God means reverence

||||||||||||||||||||||||||||||||||||||||||

HISTORICAL SNAPSHOT

Henry Smith (1560–1591) was commonly called the "Silver-tongued Preacher" and "the prime preacher of the nation" by his contemporaries. He was from a well-to-do family who studied under Richard Greenham, with whom he resided.

for Scripture. Thus, private Bible reading is an essential practice and a mark of godliness. Serving Him means obedience to His Word. The heart-imbedded Word fosters an ever-deepening receptivity to God, as it determines and judges the estate of the soul.

The Bible was a constant companion for the Puritan, either in hand or in heart: the godly were encouraged to muse, read, hear, and talk to others of God's Word. To understand what was read required a dependence on the Holy Spirit and His illuminating work. This God-given activity brought clarity, conviction, and questions that concerned the soul. Prayer and meditation accompanied their regular reading of the Scriptures, which was closely followed by conference.

Private Bible reading has a circular relationship with the Word heard: the sermon. The sermon is God's Word communicated and should be viewed as God's Word. Sermons today may not be as long as Puritan sermons, which were typically an hour, and pastors may not be able to assume we know our Bibles as well. Yet sound preaching continues to emphasize the centrality of the Bible in the Christian life. Sermons ought to be understood, remembered, and applied to personal living.

Sermons are an ordinary vehicle of grace and a chief means for conversion and growth in godliness. As John Owen asserted, "The first and principal duty of a pastor is to feed the flock by diligent preaching of the word."[3] Pastors should be keenly aware of the stylistic devices and literary qualities found in the Bible as they examine the biblical texts.

||||||||||||||||||||||||||||||||||||

HISTORICAL SNAPSHOT

John Owen (1616–1683) was a theologian and minister who was called by some "the Calvin of England" and by others "the prince of the English divines." At age twenty-six, his forty-one-year writing career began and would yield more than eighty works. In writing on the spiritual life, this theological giant advocated renovating grace.

Pastors craft their sermons to be plainly worded, down to earth, well navigated in sound doctrine and practice, understood by all, and delivered with passion. To preach God's Word diligently, pastors were to have "a kind of spiritual heat in the heart." Sermons are delivered not from mere memory, but from meditation and experience. Pastors need to preach first to their own heart and be mindful of their own spiritual growth process or they might not preach as effectively to others. As the feeder of the flock, a pastor would be ineffective if a sermon had no relevance or application in his own life. Hearers needed the same relevance and resonance in order to grow alert to the Holy Spirit's movements of power and comfort and God's voice of guidance and direction in their own life situations and circumstances.

Pastors labored to present these messages in memorable ways. The use of alliteration, numbers, emphatically used words, a variety of references to wildlife, storms and nautical images, creation, and everyday-life examples served to facilitate application and remembrance of the sermon's truths. One or two sermons were preached each Sunday and Puritans were known to flock eagerly to hear them. When given the opportunity, and it was often, Puritans would enjoin in sermon gadding, visiting one church and then another to listen to another's sermon.

The preached Word was most remembered when methodically delivered. Preston asserts that failure to preach without method was equivalent to putting "water into a sieve that will run out."[4] Pastors presented biblical truths to their congregants in ways that appealed to their hearers' spiritual hunger. The posture of receiving a sermon was not a passive experience. Four tools were employed by those who sat under the teaching of their pastors: listening, note-taking, repeating the sermon, and conference.

LISTENING

Listening to the sermon was like meditating upon Scripture, and as with meditation, it was not effortless. Attentive and engaged listening helped ensure the sermon message took root in the listener.

Pastors worked carefully to foster the hearing of sermons and to make them as memorable as possible. Richard Rogers references two other means that maximize hearing—meditation and conference: "For

HISTORICAL SNAPSHOT

Richard Rogers (c. 1550–1618) was a Church of England clergyman and author. His set of "daily devotions" for a godly life was expanded and became the work for which he is best known, *Seven Treatises*. His diary reveals details of his own personal devotions and his concern with manifesting living the godly life.

hearing of the word read and preached, doth little profit, where it is not joined with preparation to hear reverently and attentively, and where it is not mused on after, yea, and as occasion shall offer, conferred of also."[5]

The faithful of the congregation were attentive listeners as well as devoted note-takers. Observant listening fostered the ability to pen notes on the sermon, which prolonged one's engagement with the Word heard, and provided material for future and further conversations.

SERMON NOTE-TAKING

Equipped with paper and writing utensils, Puritans characteristically took sermon notes. The following week was typically spent reflecting and meditating on what had been heard by referring to these notes. In a funeral sermon by Edmund Calamy for Lady Anne Walker, she is commended as a constant recorder of sermons who wrote them in her heart as well as in her book. Her life was an exact commentary on the sermons heard.[6]

||||||||||||||||||||||||||||||||||||||

HISTORICAL SNAPSHOT

Edmund Calamy (1600–1666) was a clergyman, an ejected minister, and a popular and outspoken preacher. Richard Baxter notes that Calamy was "much valued and followed by the London ministers, as their guide; and many frequently met at his house." His life reflected one committed to national reform.

Sermon notes, when joined with reflections from other readings and personal experiences, fosters a life of piety and godliness. Both men and women are encouraged to be supplied with a stock of sermons: "We must do with sermons, as the tradesmen do with the money they get; some of it they lay out for their present use, and some they lay up against the time of sickness."[7] Note-taking was a tool used for recording that which was necessary to capture in the heart and mind of a Puritan believer: God's Word.

REPEATING THE SERMON

The Lord's Day was sacred to the Puritans. After hearing the sermon, the "food of the soul," they spent portions of the rest of the day secluded with their private devotions, catechisms, family Bible reading, and sermon notes.

Sometimes they ventured to one another's homes or their minister's to join in repeating the content and heads of the sermons heard earlier that day. John Preston cites repeating sermons as a method where "one thing is linked to another. And this is needful because we have more than a natural forgetfulness in good things."[8] Repeating the sermon is a distinct practice from the discipline of conference and may be focused more intently on the major points of a sermon rather than a discussion on its content. Isaac Ambrose exhorts his readers to "repeat what we have heard, and confer of it, and examine the Scriptures about the truth of it."[9] Repeating

|||||||||||||||||||||||||||||||||||||||||

HISTORICAL SNAPSHOT

Isaac Ambrose (1604–1664) was a Church of England clergyman and author. His lengthy *Media* is a treatise on sanctification that addresses spiritual practices for a believer to grow in grace and intimate union with Christ.

the sermon serves as a precursor to another method of remembering and then applying what was heard: the practice of conference.

CONFERENCE

Though conference was employed in a variety of contexts, many of the biblical truths that stimulated questions, concerns, and godly conversations were gleaned from sermons or from one's private Bible reading. Conference is a means to deepen spiritual knowledge through conversations "either with ministers of God. Our equals. Or others."[10] Conference is among the responsibilities of a pastor. Richard Baxter, a Puritan pastor, observes, "I have found by experience, that some ignorant persons, who have been so long unprofitable hearers, have got more knowledge and remorse of conscience in half an hour's close discourse, than they did from ten years public preaching."[11] In conference, one has "an opportunity to set all home for the conscience and the heart."[12]

When exercised among fellow Christians, conference functioned as an important part of the Puritan's spiritual life. Meetings

|||||||||||||||||||||||||||||||||||||||||

HISTORICAL SNAPSHOT

Richard Baxter (1615–1691) received a scanty education yet became of national renown as an influential pastor and author. *The Reformed Pastor* addressed pastoral neglect, but the gain from its wisdom for life is not limited to pastors.

at one another's homes to discuss the Bible or sermons heard the previous week included times to confer over the spiritual state of their souls. Thus, pastors would conference in direct face-to-face meetings and encourage conference in indirect ways as a tool by which the words of their sermons were remembered among congregants.

Sermons often stir a curious pondering of one's own sanctification or position before God, curious enough to seek answers and counsel. Pastors know well that biblical preaching alone is insufficient to set truths deeply in the heart. Questions about God's Word still arise.

One of the primary ways God reveals Himself is through special revelation: the Bible. With over forty authors from different walks of life covering a period of over 1,500 years, the primary message of God's plan in redemptive history is consistent. Through the completed work of Jesus the Christ by the power of God's Spirit, His story is preserved for us. Who is this God who is called Father? This Son who was crucified and was raised to life for the forgiveness of sin and the promise of life? This Spirit who helps us understand the Scriptures and through whom we see evidence of God working in the world? The process and progress of such knowledge can only come through God freely granting it.

The Trinity's commitment to a strengthening relationship and witness-bearing transformation is accomplished by its abiding in us. Our ability to recognize this indwelling and to desire that the goodness, grace, and kindness of Christ reign in us is accomplished by God's Spirit, who manifests this work in and through us. Regular and consistent time in God's Word must be accompanied by ways to get God's Word into us, such as biblical meditation and godly conversations. If we come away from having read, heard, or conversed on God's Word with a greater love for God and those who bear His image, then we have read, heard, remembered, and lived His Word well.

In conjunction with our private Bible reading, Bible-based sermons support, affirm, challenge, and cause us to wrestle with our understanding of God's Word, as we continue to draw more connections between various parts of the Bible. They help guide us to a more solid knowledge of God, a more intimate relationship with Christ, and a deeper dependence on His Spirit for living out His truths and thus, affirm the Bible's reliability and divine authorship.

The mutually empowering relationship between private Bible reading and the sermon helps to maintain the ability to impact corporate values and personal Christlikeness. This is possible when pastors heed their God-given calling to read, study, interpret well, apply sound theology, communicate biblical truth, and live out God's Word, and when hearers listen, retain, embed in the heart, and live out these truths. The resulting church-wide growth in biblical literacy yields greater potential for Christian spiritual transformation, the process of growing in grace and godliness that impacts one's soul and one soul to another.

Most Americans believe the Bible is a sacred text. It continues to top the best-seller list, with nine out of ten adults in America owning a Bible. Readership, however, lags behind ownership, especially among the youngest adults. Though more people are reporting stable Bible-reading habits, one of the groups with the largest decrease is millennials, those born between 1984 and 2002. This group will become proportionately larger in the coming years. For most of us, the number one reason Bible reading gets pushed to the side is busyness. Busyness can include the responsibilities of life, but be aware also of attitudes that rob us of the time to get into God's Word and for the Word to get into us: the magnetism of entitlement, pleasure, entertainment, boredom, unbelief, and an inflated view of self.

Bible reading is essential, requiring time and focus, and a humble willingness to be changed, but how we approach it is critical as well.

- If daily reading of God's Word becomes a duty, a mechanical rulebook thinking will result.
- God's Word does give us guidance, but we can mistakenly read it for guidance just for that day in a horoscope or Ouija board way.
- God's precepts help us with our problems, but a crisis management model encourages reading the Bible for miracle cures.
- Seeking encouragement from God's Word is important, yet this view can wrongly lead to a daily pick-me-up attitude.
- Where the Bible offers wisdom and insight, an academic approach can focus merely on mastering facts.[13]

The above misconstrued tendencies contribute little toward biblical literacy and Christian spiritual transformation. Proper Bible reading maintains a biblical worldview, having a God-centered view of reality.

One of the most effective ways to encourage Bible reading is to teach the Word of God, its necessity for knowing God and how this impacts our spiritual growth, and to be an example of what that looks like. Christopher Wright asserts that sermons are essential, and there is much at risk when teachers are "absent, false, or unfaithful."[14] The spiritual nourishment of God's Word is our sustenance. The Word of God, confirmed by God's Spirit, matures and sanctifies the people of God.[15] Where "there is no faithful love, and no knowledge of God," but instead, immorality, injustice, and idolatry, Hosea (4:1–2) and Amos (8:11) fault the lack of a knowledge of God. Our Christian witness is compromised to the extent that there is little or no observable difference between how believers and nonbelievers live their lives. Without good teaching, Christians either do not know or forget the metanarrative in which they are a participant in the story of what God has done, is doing, and promises to do. As Wright points out, of the qualifications for elders of the church, all address the character of that person except one. Which one? "Able to teach" and "encourage with sound teaching" (1 Timothy 3:2 and Titus 1:9), to be an able (and enabled) teacher of God's Word.

Bruce Bickel states the following problem that he later asserts can be remedied by the Puritans' approach to preaching,

> The picture of the one who preaches the Word from the pulpit as a doer of the Word appears to be dimming. . . . Many "share" rather than "preach," pray rather than pronounce blessings, and perform under a clouded vision of their ministry because they have no clear conviction about the nature of preaching. They do not see clearly the unique and supernatural nature of preaching because they do not see clearly the unique and supernatural nature of Holy Scripture.[16]

Both pastors and hearers must understand the significance and gravity of preaching: to teach the Word of God. Sermon study and preparation require a deep investment of time and a posture of dependency on God's Spirit to be enamored and infused by the riches of God's Word and to allow these to be made visible. Most in our churches have little idea what it means to live out the truth of God's Word. Consider how God's Word helps one live with devotion and purpose, navigate the mundane, stand against temptation or injustice, forgive in a challenging relationship, and engage in meaningful conversations with others.

Sound biblical teaching provokes the listener to wrestle with the truth and to be inquisitive of God's ways. Good teaching inspires attentive listening. Here are a few helpful suggestions for a closer listen to sermons:

- Listen expectantly for Christ preached from God's Word.
- Be prepared to take notes, whether hardcopy handouts are provided or not. These can be filed together or taped to a page in a personal journal, in sequence with journaling, for reviewing and highlighting personal takeaways.
- Note-take on mobile devices but only if you are not tempted to click on an app or check your emails when doing so.
- Meet together with others over coffee or lunch to discuss your takeaways from the message.
- Encourage your small group leader to facilitate conversations at the gathered meetings with well-framed questions or prompts.

Good teaching invites hearers to search the Scriptures and ask questions. It refrains from using the eloquent speech or the lacing of so many entertaining stories and anecdotes that the Word of God is not clearly presented.

The percent of Americans who report Bible skepticism, believing the Bible is "just another book written by men," is increasing.[17] Additionally, a lack of spiritual maturity and commitment to God on the part of congregations can be frustrating for pastors. Nevertheless, as David Kinnaman, president of Barna Research, has mentioned: We need to be encouraged by our pastors to "keep reaching for the Bible and to trust its words, not blindly, but with the confidence of true study and authentic questions."[18] This study and questioning, along with seeking applications to life circumstances, are accentuated when addressed in private spiritual conversations.

CHAPTER 4

"A Kind of Paradise": When Souls Were Refreshed

*For, next to heaven itself, our meeting together here,
is a kind of Paradise, the greatest pleasure of the
world is, to meet with those here, whom we shall
ever live with in Heaven.*

Richard Sibbes

I wish you more pause than fast forward.

Amy Krouse Rosenthal and Tom
Lichtenheld, *I Wish You More*, 18.

Conference as a means of grace involves both the Word of God and care for one another as souls. The biblical support for its exercise is found throughout Scripture in both the Old and New Testaments. As mentioned earlier, Malachi 3:16 was often cited by Puritans as biblical support of conference: "At that time those who feared the LORD spoke to one another. The LORD took notice and listened. So a book of remembrance was written before Him for those who feared THE LORD and had high regard for His name." Psalm 66:16 supports the charge to give one another's souls a visit, drop in your knowledge, and impart your experiences to each other. Thomas Watson describes the benefit holy conference offers when the apostle Paul seeks mutual edification among the saints in Ephesians 4:29: "Good conference enlightens the mind when it is ignorant; warms it when it is frozen; settles it when it is wavering."[1] Christians are to consider all opportunities for good discourse when they walk together and sit for a meal together. This makes their eating and drinking be to the glory of God (1 Corinthians 10:31). What makes it a communion of saints is the conference that graces these times. Both Old and New Testament verses such as these serve as the grounds and motivation for godly conversations. Engaging in conference results in minds being challenged and souls becoming attentive to one another.

Combining biblical interpretation and care for souls together in conversations furthers one's understanding of Scripture and its application toward growth of godliness in community. These discussions foster a level of discourse that can reach deep into the life of persons engaged in them.

Conference is instructive and enlightening as both biblical knowledge and life experience are promoted. There exists a complementarity between the two, with each requiring the other for greatest effect. One's growth in biblical knowledge and the sharing of that knowledge in conversation is expressed in words, in life, and in community.

|||||||||||||||||||||||||||||||||

HISTORICAL SNAPSHOT

John Downame (1571–1652) was a Church of England clergyman, theologian, and author. He published treatises, biblical concordances, collections of sermons, and wrote ten books. Among the best known are *The Christian Warfare* and *A Guide to Godliness, or a Treatise of a Christian Life.*

The experiences of others on the Christian pilgrimage are invaluable in caring for our souls and understanding how to live out the Word in everyday life. The Puritan pastor John Downame described conference as a means of grace that strengthens and increases faith, grounded in the book of Job and Paul's words in Romans 14:1:

> Holy conference with our godly brethren; for hereby those which are falling are confirmed, and the weary hands and weak knees strengthened, as Eliphaz speaks, Job 4:3–4. And those who are weak in faith are comforted and established with the godly instructions, profitable exhortations and sweet consolations of those who are more strong. And therefore the Apostle Paul exhorts those who had attained

unto a great measure of faith, that they admit such as were weak into their company to be made partakers of their Christian conferences, to the end that hereby they might be more and more strengthened and confirmed.[2]

Indeed, such advantages of empathy, encouragement, and direction are inherent for those engaged in conference.

Is it any wonder that conversations of this kind can impact many souls?

Yet biblical and ministerial support for conference does not always ensure the practice of it. In 1658 a company of fifteen ministers of Wight and Southampton "seriously and sadly" assessed the ignorance of many in their congregations, exhorting them to allow opportunities for these pastors to meet in conference with them in "this service of your souls."[3] They were confident of the positive outcomes of such a venture and willingly invested their time and attention to its promotion.

Translated into over two hundred languages, generations have read John Bunyan's *Pilgrim's Progress*. Through his characters, Christian and Hopeful, Bunyan illustrated the plight of Christians who backslide from faith. Having successfully come to their journey's end, Hopeful asked how backsliding occurred. Of the nine points given, Bunyan listed these as third and fourth: "They shun the company of lively and warm Christians," and "After that they grow cold to public duty, as hearing, reading, godly conference, and the like."[4] Christian's inclusion of the lack of

||||||||||||||||||||||||||||||||||||||||||

HISTORICAL SNAPSHOT

John Bunyan (1628–1688) was one of the great figures of seventeenth-century Puritanism. He was sent to prison for preaching without official rights from the king. His prison terms lasted for twelve years, during which he wrote a number of books, including his autobiography, *Grace Abounding to the Chief of Sinners*, and *Pilgrim's Progress*.

conference as a cause of spiritual decline reveals its importance. How great the need to confer with one another's souls on spiritual matters! That need transcends any historical period and is as relevant today.

Over the past number of years, I have had the privilege of teaching a course titled "Puritan Theology" at Biola University. This course focuses on tracing the history of Protestant spiritual formation from Martin

Luther and John Calvin to the English Puritans and acquaints students with the history, theology, and theological influences. It emphasizes the doctrinal distinctives of the Puritan movement and includes the reading of primary sources and the exercising of a variety of means of grace from that era. One is conference. Chapter 5 will help show the connection between conference and the Bible or sermons, but for now, note these student reflections from their exercise of conference.

Conference provides for aspirations. When we share how we reflect on our lives and the working that God has done in us through His Word, how they've helped us to go forward and become better in the Christian way, we are exposing our souls. This type of exposure is sincere and comforting. In the way of conferencing, we are not just reciting God's Word but making it personal and sharing the way that it's transformed our lives, which I think helps stir the souls of others, drawing them nearer to Christ, becoming better acquainted with Him, so that they too can be assured and believe in the promises of God's Word.

Katrina C.

The Puritan practice of conferencing has changed my own views of what meeting and spending time in fellowship should look like. Before learning about conferencing, the time I spent in fellowship was more of listening to each other talk about what God was doing in our lives, reading a bit of Scripture and discussing what it meant before moving on to coffee and talking about other things. But for Puritans, the practice of conferencing meant having intentional time with one another where they would spend time learning about each other. The question "how is your soul" has quickly become my favorite thing to hear. It shows the care fellow believers have for me and returning the question to hear about their relationship with God has led to my favorite conversations about God.

Victoria P.

These comments begin to reveal how conference can meet a current need.

The following chapters address different contexts in which conference may be exercised. They will help cultivate your ability to be the voice of Jesus and to manifest His presence in mutually beneficial conversations. Feel free to jump to the chapter that most grabs your attention, but the added value is in returning to other chapters as our own life roles often overlap or you have friends in another context with whom you can grow to better understand and empathize.

Further features of conference are presented in Chapter 5. Beginning in that chapter you will find the following section titles, each containing the words *Soul-to-Soul*. These words serve as a descriptor and a reminder that conference is a communal activity and rhythm that is intended to cultivate conversations between people at the most important level: their souls. A brief description for each section title is given:

- Soul-to-Soul Purpose—Conference in context
- Soul-to-Soul Perspective—Updating conference for today
- Soul-to-Soul Participants—Conference participants
- Soul-to-Soul Perks—Advantages of exercising conference
- Soul-to-Soul Paucity—Losses by the absence of conference
- Soul-to-Soul Preparation—Alerts to consider when conferencing
- Soul-to-Soul Prompts—Tiered questions, prompts, and considerations that stimulate conference at these levels:
  - ⊚ Informational
  - ⊚ Transitional
  - ⊚ Transformational

Chapters 6 through 11 describe the benefits and application of conference in different configurations of groups (that is, small groups, parents and children, marriage partners, pastors with seekers and believers, pastors with pastors, and those engaged in distance conferencing). These chapters will offer more specific evidence of the application of conference, though they are broadly summarized here.

1. SOUL CARE

Time and attention should be given in conference to the advancement of biblical knowledge as well as to exploring the states of souls. Downame revealed what can be involved when one examines the state of one's soul: one may "seriously examine our estate in the audit of conscience, and as in God's presence, how it stands between him and us, and whether it is thriving and growing better, or decaying and waxes worse in spiritual graces, and in the practice of Christian and holy duties."[5] The intersection of life experiences with the biblical truths that inform those experiences comes to the fore in conference.

||||||||||||||||||||||||||||||||||

HISTORICAL SNAPSHOT

Richard Sibbes (1577–1635) was one of the most influential Puritan divines, a celebrated pastor, preacher, and theologian. He was dedicated to providing biblical theology and making it relevant to the godly layperson.

The divine element of conference cannot be ignored. God may ordain an apparent spiritual weakness or void for the very purpose of seeking out another pilgrim to meet and fill that need. His intent may be for the uniting of one with another for the benefit of more—those gathered and God Himself.

Richard Sibbes suggested that God appoints specific others to help us address our doubts and questions. As he observed, "Many go mourning a great part of their days in a kind of sullenness this way, because that they do not open their estate to others."[6]

2. BIBLICAL LITERACY

Conference provides growth in knowledge that attracts not only those who are well versed in Scripture but also those who find themselves at any point on the biblical literacy spectrum. To those who are more biblically literate, it gives them opportunities to come alongside in sharing their knowledge as well as experience in the Christian journey. It is not an arena to show one's spiritual prowess but to invest in others' lives and offer counsel for their pilgrimage. For those whose biblical literacy is lower, conference is an opportunity to glean from those more spiritually knowledgeable and experienced. It is a gathering for all with a humble desire for growth and community.

Minds are challenged by the truths found in the Scriptures. Sibbes compared the biblical discussions involved in conference to the seed that eventually brings forth a tree,[7] and Isaac Ambrose wrote of the comfort to be gained in Scripture because it strengthens our communion with the "God of all consolation."[8]

It is right that believers glean insights from their Bible reading or sermon notes individually and then intentionally draw together for the purpose of seeking clarity and relevance. After all, as Ambrose noted, it was so modeled in Acts 17:11, where the Bereans were said to search the Scriptures daily regarding Paul's teaching. Ambrose suggested poetically that "after we have been in the garden of spices and have felt the savor of Christ's ointments in church-assemblies, let us take some of the flowers away with us, and smell them again and again. *Repeating, conferring, examining the word,* is as pounding of spices, that will make them smell more."[9]

There is a reverence for Scripture we may recapture from the Puritans, and a spiritual nourishing that comes from employing conference.

3. MEMORIZATION AID

Conference assists the memory, and memory is intrinsically linked with growth in understanding Scripture. If the Word of God is to be the constant guide on which one relies for direction in the conduct of life, then knowing it is basic and crucial. John Udall, an English clergyman, proposed conference be used to double-check one's sermon notes as well as to be reminded of key points, to the mutual edification of all involved.[10]

This means of grace ensures that nothing of importance is lost in transmission. The mutual edification is lost without conference with one another. Stimulated, shared recollection of God's Word is an avenue for expanding spiritual knowledge.

‖‖‖‖‖‖‖‖‖‖‖‖‖‖‖‖‖‖‖‖‖‖‖‖‖‖‖‖‖‖‖‖‖

HISTORICAL SNAPSHOT

John Udall (c. 1560–1592/93) was an author and eloquent Puritan preacher. He has been called "one of the most fluent and learned of puritan controversialists." *Obedience to the Gospell,* a volume of expository sermons, was intended for "the congregation of Christ's people, embracing the truth of the Gospel."

4. MINISTERIAL CARE

The ministry of preaching alone is insufficient. Conference may be more time intensive, but its benefits are undeniable. Richard Baxter argued that those "who have been so long unprofitable hearers, have got more knowledge and remorse of conscience in half an hour's close discourse, than they did from ten years public preaching."[11]

Spiritual conversations allow for a type of interaction between clergy and laity that furthers the ability of ministers to know the members of their congregations. This one-with-one time gives opportunity to plumb the depths of a person's spiritual formation with the hope that their pastor can better individualize the care given to them. This interaction develops and deepens the relationships necessary to tailor a pastor's efforts in communicating to, praying for, and overall ministering to his congregation.

In sum, conference is a means of grace that affords opportunities to ask questions and to converse with the spiritually mature. These meaningful, care-inducing, empathy-raising conversations connect knowledge with experiences. It is not limited to any particular group of people. There is no gender, literacy, or class distinction. In conference there should be no discrimination. Through it, many have been given the opportunity for personal spiritual recalibration that will have a direct impact on themselves, their families, community, culture, and society. No one matures alone. As a once widely accepted, practiced, and profitable means of grace among the godly, conference as encouraged and enjoyed then is fully needed now.

CHAPTER 5

PEEK TO PIQUE: FEATURES OF CONFERENCE

*We lose the benefit we might have by the
conversation of wise men for want of the art of being
inquisitive.*

Matthew Henry on Proverbs 20:5

*By putting questions to others, sometimes to teach,
and sometimes to be taught; and this do, if possible,
in all occasional meetings, and worldly discourses;
mix with it sweet truth that God has taught thee.*

Thomas Shepard, *Subjection to
Christ in All His Ordinances*

Conference enjoys some similarities with ordinary practices people might do together. Discussion might be one. Conference is certainly a type of discussion, but where it differs is in its manner and purpose.

‖‖‖

HISTORICAL SNAPSHOT

Thomas Shepard (1605–1649) was a minister in both England and New England. He was silenced by Bishop Laud before going into hiding and eventually sailing to New England. Shepard was instrumental in founding Harvard College in 1636.

SOUL-TO-SOUL PURPOSE

Discussion may be the consideration or examination of an argument or a talk intended to reach a solution, but conference is informal conversation, a casual yet genuine exchange of thoughts focused on spiritual matters. It incorporates an attentiveness to one another's words, thoughts, and lives, and has its purpose in connecting biblical truths with life experiences. In this way, participants are strengthened and encouraged and better able to recognize God's work in their lives.

Private conference shares strong parallels with the practice of spiritual direction in its intentionality to set aside time and space to focus on God's movements, promptings, and nudges. Of special focus is how these are woven together in a person's life. Dallas Willard states, "Spiritual direction was understood by Jesus, taught by Paul, obeyed by the early church, followed with excesses in the medieval church, narrowed by the Reformers, recaptured by the Puritans, virtually lost in the modern church."[1] This recaptured spiritual direction is found in conference. Spiritual direction is typically focused on one individual and his or her spiritual state, whereas the conversations in conference can be applied to an individual as well as a range of small-group sizes. The main emphasis lies in the coming together of people in private meetings to have an opportunity to "set all [biblical truths] home for the conscience and the heart," while conversing over the state of their souls.

This is risky. We would rather be distracted from the realities of life and our need for life-giving, relational community. It is risky to allow another into the safe places of our lives. These safe places provide a secure and protected space, but without a trusted community, untruths that we hold, harbor, and hide in our safe places can be expressed in life-denying actions and behaviors that reflect a devaluing of self, others, and God.

SOUL-TO-SOUL PERSPECTIVE

Listening, questioning, and responding are foundational to effective conference. Participants are encouraged to "listen diligently unto that which is spoken, in a desire to learn."[2] Many elements compete with and frustrate our cultivating a desire to listen well. Most are centered on our own wants, wishes, and agendas. To develop good and careful listening,

- Eliminate competing distractions. Turn off cell phones and personal devices. In a small group, collect the devices in a box and charge a fee for use during your small-group time. This may become a new revenue stream for supporting a ministry.
- Find that sweet spot in your time together, such as the best day, time of day, or length of time for a given conference session.
- Look at the speaker's eyes. This is the most powerful form of human connection.[3] Note if your own dart off in another direction or if your mind travels off subject.
- Do not worry about your response. It will be better if you keep listening intently. The Bible says it is foolishness and a disgrace to give an answer before listening (Proverbs 18:13).
- Continue listening with the intent to incorporate what you have heard into interceding prayer.
- Jot key words down on a piece of paper to help you remember. Again, avoid using mobile devices; it takes away from the humanness of the moment.

Empathy is developed when listening is done well. This can lead to discerning and insightful questions.

Well-framed questions or prompts are not asked for the sake of asking questions. That would be purposeless. Instead, they are posed for the purpose of mutual understanding and growth. God does not put two people together for the benefit of one. He does it for the benefit of both those in conversation and Himself, for His glory. Well-framed questions and prompts establish a place and points of contact and allow us to begin to hear a story. Notice the mutuality in one's questions breeding questions in others, as Puritan preacher Richard Sibbes observed:

> Here is the benefit of holy conference and good speeches. One thing draws on another, and that draws on another, till at length the soul be warmed and kindled with the consideration and meditation of

heavenly things. That that is little in the beginning may bring forth great matters.[4]

These types of conversations include mutual engagement and mutual response. Responding is a process of thinking, rethinking, and refining thoughts. We must allow ourselves and others to process thoughts to most clearly articulate them. This is often facilitated by further questions as trust and empathy are built.

It is helpful to self-assess the quality of your intimacy, vulnerability, transparency, and presence before and with God. The tendency to avoid God, to place spending time with Him as a low priority, or to feel uncomfortable at the thought of Him wanting to be with you corresponds with an uneasiness to address deep matters of the heart with others. Our attentiveness with and before God can mirror our ability to be attentive with and before others. At the same time, our desire to be present and attentive to others can mirror our desire to be present and attentive to God.

SOUL-TO-SOUL PARTICIPANTS

The following chapters will show various contexts in which conference can be exercised. Pastors may conference with other pastors. Pastors may conference with those in their congregations. Small groups of believers may conference among themselves. Spouses may conference together. Parents may conference with their children, young and adult. And it is even possible to conference at a distance. The common thread among these expressions is a desire for meaningful conversations on spiritual matters that impact how one is to live out the biblical truth of God with us.

The honesty and transparency required for conference to be most effective demands that groups be of a reasonable size. It is difficult to promote truthful and candid conversations in large groups. Trusted relationships are borne of honest dialogue and secured acceptance. This can best be nurtured in groups numbering two to ten. The numerical figure is second to the qualitative aspects of any size group, so the gauge is not so much the number of participants but the quality of conversation toward continued transformation.

SOUL-TO-SOUL PERKS

Puritan pastor Richard Stock reminded us that God regards and rewards godly conversations; they serve as "an encouragement for God's children, that are talking together of good things, a strong motive to move them to confer together of good things."[5] Conversations are not unnoticed by God.

New learning and the instilling of biblical truths takes place in conference alongside the confirming of truths experientially in our lives. What makes conversations

HISTORICAL SNAPSHOT

Richard Stock (1569–1626) was a famed puritan minister in London. His commentary on Malachi was published posthumously in 1641.

transformational is what happens to those who make it their responsibility to engage with God and others in meaningful conference that highlights God's involvement, presence, and power. With a more accurate view of God, participants are able to recognize the work of the Holy Spirit as the agent of change and how He often uses others as conduits of His work.

SOUL-TO-SOUL PAUCITY

The Puritans would describe the downheartedness experienced in life as a "decay of care, zeal, and watchfulness"—polluted thoughts, misspoken words that were unsavory and unedifying, and actions that did not adorn the doctrine of the gospel. If one's "spiritual relish of God's word is very insipid," the power of its authority is reduced, thus one becomes "unready to anything that is good." In turn one's blessings and comfort are diminished.

In *Pilgrim's Progress,* John Bunyan described an additional pitfall from the lack of conference—the lack of correction when a proposed biblical interpretation is questionable, which can lead to unbiblical rationale for ungodly attitudes or behavior. The continued state of error found in Formalist and Hypocrisy is attributed to the absence of conversations that might enlighten and educate. This lack is echoed in two of the six woes found in Isaiah 5: Moral confusion in calling evil good and good evil, and the autonomy found in being wise in one's own eyes. Being "spiritual" without a growing and anchored knowledge of God and His Word can result in a theology of conflicting beliefs and a lifestyle inconsistent with reflecting and expressing biblical truth.

SOUL-TO-SOUL PREPARATION

Conferencing with others does not come naturally for most people. With an awareness of the need for it in our communities, greater personal dependence on God's Spirit, and the shared wisdom and experience of Christ-hearted individuals, it is worth the investment of our mental, emotional, and spiritual attention and time. The self-preparation for it requires a steady walk with God, learning more about Him and growing closer to Him through an effective study of His Word. If you walk away from reading His Word without sensing a change in your relationship with Him or others, you have not read it well.

HISTORICAL SNAPSHOT

Richard Greenham (c. 1535–c. 1594) was a tireless preacher and physician of souls. "A Profitable treatise containing a direction for the reading and understanding of the Holy Scriptures" focuses on getting into God's Word, so that His Word can get into us.

Conference requires not only a heart for God, but for people. To many of us, people have become irritants or interruptions in our daily pursuit of our own agenda. Richard Greenham warns that individuals must attend conference "in love without anger, envy, or desire of victory."[6] Participating in conference requires a loving humility that is void of personal agendas and prideful exchanges. This allows more discerning and insightful questions to be asked and responses to be given.

Conference also involves silence. A common hurdle is the inevitable silence that occurs in meaningful spiritual conversations. Silence should not be seen as "dead space." Lulls in a discussion might seem awkward or be interpreted to mean that nothing is happening. Silence is actually a crucial element in a conversational rhythm. To be comfortable even and especially in the silences grows trust among listeners and allows needed moments for thoughts to become spoken words and body language.

As such, conference will be a challenging endeavor, but a humble corrective can be found in spending time in a classic means of grace: silence and solitude with ourselves and God. Where silence and solitude are uncomfortable for us is where God is nurturing the shadow side of our spiritual growth. We are learning about ourselves and learning that being alone does not have to mean being lonely. It becomes a time to brainstorm with yourself. Silence and solitude break the seduction of image management, busyness, and delusions of self-importance, and allow us to grow our capacity for empathy and self-reflection.[7] We get to debrief with ourselves as we hear His invitation to exchange our insecurities, fears, and brokenness for God-aligned gifts of value, assurance, and healing. The closer we come to see the *imago Dei*, "the image of God," in others and ourselves, the more humbly we resonate with the shades of brokenness in our human stories. The goal is not to become an expert in exercising silence and solitude but rather to become more like Christ, as areas of our lives come into focus that need greater dependence on God.

In addition, establishing a rhythm of time spent in silence and solitude before God increases our familiarity and comfortableness with silence before others. Listening abilities are enhanced, as is one's readiness to remain engaged in silence. Learning to grow in patience and attentiveness will allow listeners to make more discreet observations of words spoken or not spoken and of body language. Spoken words become fewer yet more potent and thoughtful.

As one listens well, subsequent words or gestures can validate the other. In establishing healthy conversations, how one responds to a reply or comment is critical. Learning to accept a response without debate, explanation, or becoming defensive is vital. This includes refraining from adding one's own similar experience, which can be disguised as empathy but may actually be a blind spot to our own pridefulness. Consider these responses that validate a person's being and help facilitate the next step in a conversation:

- Look a person in the eye.
- Nod your head, signaling they have been heard.
- Smile.
- Consider any change in facial expressions.
- "Tell me more."
- "I don't fully understand. Help me to better understand."
- "That must not have been easy."
- "Thank you."
- "You may be right."

There are many ways to cultivate the types of godly conversations that aim to build, encourage, heal, and strengthen. Each of the following chapters introduces a context where conference can be practiced and explains how these contexts can be impacted by this means of grace.

The meeting together of image-bearers has challenges as well. Some of these challenges are found in Chapter 1, such as a felt fear of not belonging or feeling inadequate in Bible knowledge. Some falsely believe that everyone else has their act together and would not welcome someone who does not. And yet we persist to meet the underlying desire to be in community. Mark Zuckerberg attests to this on a leg of his Year of Travel after visiting with a group of pastors:

> I met with ministers in Waco who are helping their congregations find deeper meaning in a changing world . . . This trip has helped me understand just how important community is, and how we're all just looking for something we can trust. We may come from different backgrounds, but we all want to find purpose and authenticity in something bigger than ourselves.[8]

Community is important. The caution lies in this: our service, regular meetings, caring for one another, fun together, meeting weekly, practicing spiritual disciplines together, sharing the gospel in word and deed, eating together—each and every one of these elements, as needful and critical as they are for growth, have the potential to be empty. Until and unless these activities create a trusted environment that is conducive to having meaningful conversations, they will remain activities, expectations, and some great shared times together, but they will ultimately eclipse the kind of community and culture where the knowledge of God through His Word is furthered and souls are attended.

Prayerfully asking for the God-given desire and guidance to step into godly conversations needs to be joined with the commitment to put self aside. This commitment will allow God's involvement in growing healthy communities to be highlighted and demonstrate how important spiritual conversations are to Him, ultimately, manifesting Himself in our lives.

SOUL-TO-SOUL PROMPTS

The prompts and questions provided here come in three levels, or tiers: Informational, Transitional, and Transformational. Informational level questions are nonthreatening and do not require deep relationship; however, responses to entry-level questions can be the initial steps to fostering or establishing trust in relationships. Transitional questions move the conversation to a level that requires more thought and personal depth and engagement. These questions and prompts reflect a level of care and honesty. Transformational questions and prompts challenge people to the greatest level of transparency and trust-building. Asking permission may be necessary, as these are sacred inquiries that express care. Notice that all of the prompts require more than an affirmative or negative, yes or no response. The best questions are versatile and elicit thoughtful and substantive responses.

The following examples introduce well-framed conference prompts and questions. These are not exhaustive lists, but they are useful in assessing the level of questions you tend to pose and to assist in furthering conversations toward deeper spiritual engagement. Those found in the following chapters reflect more specifically the type of participants engaging in conference. Though each of these prompts has its Informational, Transitional, and Transformational sequence, resist rushing to the next level. It is not a race; it is a relationship.

Informational

1. What made your day a good one? What made you stop and wonder?

2. If you were to thank God for one thing in your life today, what would it be?

3. I am most fulfilled by _____.

4. What is one takeaway from your time with God in His Word today?

5. How familiar are you with the means of grace of silence and solitude?

6. What is the soul?

7. If you are with an Uber/Lyft driver: How long have you been a driver for Uber/Lyft? How did you decide to be one?

Transitional

1. Why do you think that particular event or sighting caught your attention?

2. How does being thankful cultivate a humble heart?

3. How might your being fulfilled by _____ reflect (or not reflect) God's design for your life?

4. What did God reveal about Himself? What implications are there of this truth in your relationships?

5. Whether a newbie, novice, or natural, what possibilities, fears, anxieties, or surprises might time in silence and solitude hold for you?

6. If the soul is the whole person, body and spirit, how stands it between God and your soul now?

7. Do you have a family? How is your family impacted by your driving for Uber/Lyft?[1]

Transformational

1. In the quiet moments of your day or night, what is God impressing on your soul? How does this relate to what caught your attention today?

2. Without expressing thanksgiving, our gratitude is incomplete. How would others describe your gratitude quotient? How would God describe it?

3. Paul states in Colossians 2:10 that as believers we are complete in Christ. What in your life competes with this truth?

4. What opportunity is God presenting you with to depend on His Spirit to reflect His presence and reign in your life?

5. Spend at least thirty minutes in silence and solitude and record your reflections to share at a later time.

6. The heart is the control center of the soul. It is mentioned about a thousand times in the Bible. It is that important to God. How is your heart?

7. Note a quality about your driver and affirm their value to you and to God.

---

1   Uber/Lyft drivers are some of the most ignored service providers, yet they are a captive audience, many of whom would welcome an opportunity to share their story and be heard by another's caring extension of conversation. So, remove the earbuds and invest in a short time of conference.

PART II

Conference in Various Life Contexts

CHAPTER 6

SMALL (AND DEEPER) GROUP CONFERENCES

One of my spiritual friends has been in my face and by my side.

Klaus Issler, *Wasting Time with God*

Go fast, go alone. Go far, go together.

African proverb

Conference held an important place in the life of the godly. The Puritans revived the practice of seeking spiritual guidance from one's neighbor or pastor.

SOUL-TO-SOUL PURPOSE

As a grassroots movement, Puritans often chose their peers for spiritual guidance. Perhaps they found that practicing their faith with earnestness required other like-hearted sojourners. A cluster of seventeenth-century English pastors observed "that some private Christians have a richer stock of experiences, than ministers generally have."[1] Meeting in one another's homes creates a welcoming forum to expound on the narrative from which questions and comments from our private Bible reading or sermons can be fielded.

||||||||||||||||||||||||||||||||||||||

HISTORICAL SNAPSHOT

William Laud (1573–1645) was appointed Archbishop of Canterbury in 1633. Laud unleashed a bitter persecution of Puritans, opposing the Puritan observance of the Sabbath by demanding that the *Book of Sports*, be read from every pulpit upon threat of suspension.

||||||||||||||||||||||||||||||||||||||

HISTORICAL SNAPSHOT

Roger Quatermayne was a seventeenth-century Puritan lawyer who was investigated by Archbishop Laud. A response to a warrant being served him, Quatermayne says there are "three things that made a man cheerful; a good God, a good Cause, and a good Conscience."

||||||||||||||||||||||||||||||||||||||

HISTORICAL SNAPSHOT

Nicholas Bownd (died 1613) was a Church of England clergyman and religious writer, best known for his work, *The Doctrine of the Sabbath.*

The distrust created in the mind of Archbishop of Canterbury William Laud over private conferences fueled his disdain for the gathering of Puritans "to meet together to pray, read, preach, expound God's word."[2] These suspicions further drove the persecution he imposed. In a debate, Puritan lawyer Roger Quatermayne argued that these were not instances of unlawful preaching but rather "godly conference, which every Christian man is bound to do and perform."[3] Just as they had a public duty to attend services, so it was their private duty to read and discuss Scripture—to conference.

Christians have an obligation to care for each other's spiritual health. By exercising conference together, the common and mutual goal of growth in godliness can be achieved. Coming together to discuss the Scriptures or reflections from sermon notes forms the basis for our private meetings. Nicholas Bownd challenged his readers that by "the conferring and talking with others of that which we have in the word read or heard: especially seeing both it is commended unto us in the Scripture, and also by experience we shall find the profit of it to be so great, to our selves and others."[4]

Conference involves digging into biblical texts in conjunction with conferring over the state of souls. Church of England clergyman John Rogers commented on the communion of the saints noting, "He that walks with the wise, shall be the wiser; much good may we learn, and comfort may we get, by conversing with them that be truly godly."[5] There is a clear connection between

Scripture as it relates to the state of one's soul. Submission to Scripture can be the litmus test as the counsel of Scripture determines and reveals our spiritual condition. Conference provides the safe environment for such disclosures in small groups and even in a meeting of two. Jonathan Mitchel recommends, "If you have a friend with whom you might now and then spend a little time, in conferring together, in opening your hearts, and presenting your unutterable groanings before God, it would be of excellent use."[6]

The Puritans do not provide us with a detailed instruction manual for community groups, but they do commend the benefits for both individuals and the corporate body.

SOUL-TO-SOUL PERSPECTIVE

Small groups are a biblical nonnegotiable because it is in these contexts that Christian maturity happens.[7] These meetings are indispensable for growth in Christlikeness. Though community groups can help people adapt to societal demands and pressures, they do not necessarily enable members to lead significantly different lives. Challenges, especially those resulting in genuine transformation, are either not posed or conveniently sidelined, especially if personal sacrifice or discomfort are involved. Ed Stetzer and Eric Geiger found that group attenders primarily sought comfort over accountability or correction.[8] We have become too nice, too polite.

Small groups adopt a culture of niceness when commitment-challenged attenders are constantly on the move. In an effort to keep the group intact, it is sometimes believed that rocking the boat will cause people to abandon ship. The hypersensitive, culture-inflicted fear of offending or upsetting anyone can add to the even greater internal propensity to hide one's true self, challenging our abilities to create an atmosphere and venue where free-flowing, trusted conversations become the norm. This kind of niceness contrasts the support found in conversations that enable the transformation divinely expected of us and the depth of community desired.

Additionally, someone has become too small. God. Attendees may not be encouraged to seek and explore higher goals such as a healthier sense of the transcendent that influences how one can live differently, influentially, and convincingly. Instead, the individual becomes the gauge of all things. With more attention placed on the temporal, material, and human side of spiritual experiences, the invisible and divine are marginalized. God becomes manageable and serviceable to us in meeting our needs, and He exists to assuage difficult life situations. This picture of God results from a kind of faith and teaching focused more on feelings and getting along in life than on worshipful obedience and reverence toward a transcendent God.[9] Our God reveals Himself as such in the Bible. But who knows their Bible?

Christians in small groups are too biblically and theologically illiterate. They lack a general understanding of the larger metanarratives of the Bible and instead embrace individualistic interpretations of Bible passages, placing a greater emphasis on personal significance than on implications drawn from the actual meaning of a passage. Even with an adequate understanding of the biblical text, one can still avoid the implications it has for one's own life. One can have Bible knowledge without transformation, but there is no transformation without knowledge of the Word of God. Biblical knowledge is a precursor but not a sufficient indicator of Christian living. A serious limitation of character formation exists when Bible knowledge does not translate into a transformed life. The casualties of biblical illiteracy and insufficient transformation can be many: families, Christian communities, the disillusioned and post-churched, interested seekers, the lost, and the next generation.

The disparity between knowledge of God's Word and observable differences of transformed lives is symptomatic of the need for engagement with the Word in conjunction with care for one another's souls. Knowledge must be incorporated into the core of our beings. George Gallup Jr. and D. Michael Lindsay present this challenge:

> We need to work toward closing the gap between belief and practice—we need to turn professed faith into lived-out faith. What is called for is not new communities, new strategies or position papers; we need nothing less than changed hearts.[10]

Until we recognize the need to engage biblical knowledge at the heart level in community, genuine Christian spiritual transformation will be meager. Conversations connecting knowledge with the heart and soul in conference consequently affect the way we live.

The above observations on small groups can be applied to any number of groups, whether composed of participants drawn together by life stage, roles, ministry functions, or family. The spiritual strength that a small-group community is able to achieve and maintain is in direct relationship to the depth of intimacy realized.

SOUL-TO-SOUL PARTICIPANTS

Conference can be as planned and structured as a small-group meeting or as unplanned and unstructured as a serendipitous conversation with another. Men and women who engage in conference desire for their transforming lives to continue on a trajectory that impacts self and others, and they know community accomplishes this aim. Indeed, researchers Todd Heatherton and Patricia Nichols found that community was strongly associated with successful change.[11] Encouragement and challenges shared in healthy communities can grow our dependence upon God. They are strong catalysts for transformation.

It would be easy to assume when groups of men and women meet, whether co-ed or grouped by gender, that each member would have a measure of biblical literacy. Biblical literacy, however, was not a qualifier when Puritans met together. There could be a spectrum from people with little or no knowledge of the Bible to seasoned believers of more than a few decades. Interestingly, in conference a desire to know more biblical truth is stirred and long-held beliefs are corrected, supplanted with an even greater desire to know God, His Word, and His ways.

The dynamics of a group are necessarily and positively impacted by the roles assigned or assumed by its members.[12] The task-oriented leader is given permission to keep the group on task whereas the relational leader is able to read faces and nonverbal cues and listens intently to what is being said and not said. Time-keepers honor the time constraints of a meeting with firmness and grace to open and close a meeting on time. A recorder enjoys making lists, taking notes, and being involved by emailing those in the group with important information such as prayer concerns and updates. A perspective-taker is able to notice what might be missing and can make helpful suggestions to the group. While more than one role may be filled by an individual, they are best performed by many, each exercising their unique gift and sensibility corporately. Over time, as these gifts are exercised, participation, responsibility, and ownership of the group grows and the intimacy for sharing life's challenges and twists and turns deepens.

It is important to have leaders with a sound biblical and theological understanding of God's Word. Coupled with the humble attitude of being lifelong learners, leaders create an atmosphere where members feel safe to ask questions and voice the struggles of applying a biblical truth to life expressions. Leaders who cultivate this safety are able to draw out important matters from conversations. Gifted leaders have the heart and skill described in Proverbs 20:5, "Counsel in a person's heart is deep water; but a man of understanding draws it out." Matthew Henry comments that some "have a great deal in them but it is loth [reluctant] to come out. In such a case a man of understanding will draw it out as wine out of a vessel."[13]

||||||||||||||||||||||||||||||||||||

HISTORICAL SNAPSHOT

Matthew Henry (1662–1714) was a leading Nonconformist Puritan minister and distinguished devotional Bible commentator, known for his substantial *Commentary on the Whole Bible*. His ability to read, understand, and study God's Word was aided by his knowledge of Latin, Greek, and Hebrew languages learned as a child.

This requires wisdom, discernment, compassion, and patience.

There are times when "pressing into" a comment made by a group member is necessary. It could be a theological position or a behavior that is inconsistent with God's character or ways. A nonthreatening way to present this is in the form of a question, framed to require deeper thinking in response. When trust is established, any group member whose approach is Spirit-led in grace, truth, and love, and whose objective is not to condemn but to strengthen the other can add to effective conferencing. To be silent can enable another's blind spots. Asking a well-framed question instead allows for more reflective dialogue and attentiveness to each other's words and hearts, which can lead to real change while deepening respect, care, trust, and acceptance among members.

SOUL-TO-SOUL PERKS

Conference impacts those who participate in these gatherings. Within the sphere of intimacy and confidentiality, godly instruction, divine consolation, brotherly admonition, and charitable admonitions are more tenderly received. Believers grow in belief, biblical knowledge, and care for one another. Once considered to be an indication of a true Christ follower was when one "delights in the saints' company above all others, as finding a heavenly sweetness in their *conference* and society, where every one's words do savor of grace and wisdom."[14] Samuel Clarke, a Puritan pastor, adds love to this list, that participants, "though living ten or twelve miles asunder, were as intimate and familiar, as if they had been all of one household."[15]

HISTORICAL SNAPSHOT

Samuel Clarke (1599–1682) was a clergyman, an ejected minister, and a biographer. He is most famous for the biographies of clerics and noble professors, producing testimonies of Puritans of worthy moderation and examples of life.

The impact of conference exercised in small groups extended beyond the boundaries of meetings. Perhaps it was serendipitous conference that John Bunyan happened upon that proved to be a spiritual marker in his life. He repented of sin and began to live a life according to God's commandments when he encountered something that jolted him out of his complacency. He overheard a group of women talking of spiritual things:

> *I heard, but I understood not . . .* for their talk was about a new birth, the work of God on their hearts, also how they were convinced of their miserable state by nature: they talked how God had visited their souls with his love in the Lord Jesus, and with what words and promises they had been refreshed, comforted, and supported against the temptations of the Devil.

These women spoke of spiritual matters in this godly conversation, and as Bunyan overheard it, he found something new, and confessed, "They were to me as if they had found a new world."[16] Edifying talk builds others up according to their needs that it may also benefit those who are within an earshot of those who conference.

Times of peace, conflict, fellowship, learning, temptation, depression, or despair were some of the episodes of need lived in fellowship with other Christians found in Bunyan's *Pilgrim's Progress*. Comfort in the throes of death, clarity in the enigmas of life, and courage mustered amid adversity and fear were evidence of the camaraderie and community fostered by conference, but so was the simple life-promoting encouragement in renewing one's "Christian course." Conference was crucial to the lives of these pilgrims because it "made the way easy."[17] These truths are echoed by Amit Sood of the Mayo Clinic College of Medicine: "Shared feelings dilute fears, reduce the weight of a burden, and invite new ideas. The lesser the need to suppress thoughts and emotions, the greater the authenticity and health experienced in and between participants."[18]

HISTORICAL SNAPSHOT

Edmund Staunton (1600–1671) was an ejected minister. He became known as "the searching preacher," who catechized the "younger and ignorant sort of people" and "taught them also from house to house."

Samuel Clarke records the quality of care and concern Edmund Staunton extended, along with the manner of conference that he demonstrated:

> Whoever conversed with him, and was not a gainer by his heavenly discourse? His speech was always with grace, which as it argued grace in the speaker, so it was apt to work, or stir up grace in the hearers, it was ever savory, seasoned with salt, and good to the use of edifying, Eph.4.29.

What a remarkable commentary on the exercised skill of conferencing—listening to free-flowing conversations and offering substantive words of edification and grace. Such are these who "made the way easy."

Remembering one another outside of gathered times, which quickens the heart to prayerful recollection, is an added benefit. There is more mindfulness of each other in the absences when much is reaped in one another's presence.

Some modern day benefits of conference exercised in small groups are found in these reflections from former students and friends:

> Conferencing is the very act of "getting down to the good stuff" because the Gospel is too radical to stay confined to Sunday and not permeate and pervade the week that follows. They [English Puritans] have harkened my spirit back to truth and grace. Without this spiritual discipline of conferencing, and my openness to it, the conversations that have been most formative in my life would never have come to pass. I want as many of my fellow members of the body of Christ to be acquainted with the state of my soul so as to recognize when I desperately need encouragement and spurring toward the "goal, which Christ has called me heavenward." And in seeing such blessing profit from conferencing, I wish to be the very same blessing to those around me. It is the greatest blessing of God to see our unique and specific journeys as a community touched by the Gospel and biblical truth. It is the very interacting of the Holy Spirit with us, and others, that is seen most tangibly in and through conference.

> Marianna M.

The six of us meet every other week on Tuesday nights, which is what worked out best for everyone. We take breaks around holidays, but other than that we meet year round. I've had men's groups in the early morning, but there's always a sense of the impending work day that distracts me, not to mention the need to get up early, which isn't fun. We meet for about an hour and a half, more or less.

Some of us share more deeply than others, and that's fine, but we all appreciate one another and enjoy being a part of each other's lives. We've been meeting since November 2015, and it feels like as time goes on, we get to be a part of each man's journey in a meaningful way. It really does feel like each person is a novel, and we're reading a bit of the novel each time we meet. But it's much more than that, because we're involved in the story, and we can see how God works in each of our stories. I connect deeply with a couple guys, and a couple are good friends.

Elijah F.

Over dinner I met with Andrew, Natalie, and Natasha to talk about our souls. I began the conversation about what I learned at church that morning because it was a really powerful message on living in community via 1 John 1:1–4. I told them about how I am in a place where the Lord is challenging me to serve others as much as possible and not expect anything in return, which was what the message was about. I also talked about what we have been learning in Hebrews, which directly applied to the message. After I spoke, we just went around our circle commenting on what I have learned in church. Then we moved on to a period of being honest about what is going on in our hearts.

I am so unbelievably thankful for this conference I had. Our dinner conversation was one of the most honest conversations I've ever been a part of. We expressed our feelings of despair in recognizing our brokenness. . . . I listened to the deep sadness in the life of one of my friends. I heard the heart of a friend who was mad at God. I sat and listened to a friend's fear of prayer because past prayers were answered with a "No." The best part of it all was I never lost hope. The Holy Spirit is alive and working faithfully. . . . I am not a person who gives physical touch often, but my spirit let me reach out and hug my sad, beloved friends. I felt hope because I was reminded that Christ conquered all sin and brokenness on the cross, and although we love in a world of despair, we have hope. The practice of conference breaks the barrier of secrecy and loneliness and makes room for the body of Christ to do what it is called to do, and that is to love.

Paige W.

Every Sunday we've met after church for potluck, and we've discussed the sermon, tested it against Scripture, asked questions of each other and sometimes of our pastor, and have had accountability to pay attention and engage and apply the weekly sermons to daily life and work. . . . This group, and the practice of focused fellowship surrounding the sermon, has been so good for my soul. It has forced me to relearn regular spiritual disciplines of prayer, Bible reading and study, and evangelism apart from the Christian college setting. It has held me up as I've floundered at times and waxed and waned in my motivation to follow Jesus. It has provided a place to invite visitors to our church to engage further in what we heard through the Sunday service. Ultimately, conference has become a place where every person is engaged in asking questions and finding answers, and has accountability to follow Jesus throughout the week. I'm not sure what might have happened if this group had decided to spend our group times differently—perhaps with some other kind of Bible study format. Perhaps there would have been the same outcome, perhaps not. But God has certainly used conference as a powerful means of grace in my life and in those who have conferenced with me for the past year.

Alanna D.

Conference deeply fosters life-giving relationships where support, transparency, and commitment to one another are valued and embraced.

SOUL-TO-SOUL PAUCITY

Without safe places to have conversations that challenge, encourage, and spur us toward growth, community will be anemic and destined for stagnant, listless, silo-type living, consistent with these "lesses" and "fewers."

- Less reading and studying the Bible
- Less memorizing Scripture
- Less seeking God
- Less spending time with other believers
- Less interest in those outside the faith

- Less thinking and understanding of biblical truths
- Less praying for others in and outside the church
- Less praying in a group with other Christians
- Less confession and asking forgiveness of God
- Less conviction toward obedience to God
- Less involvement in church responsibilities and ministries
- Fewer significant relationships with Christians
- Fewer conversations with Christians
- Less attending worship services[19]

SOUL-TO-SOUL PREPARATION

As helpful counterexamples, here are suggestions for how to create a "loser" small group environment where conference is diminished:

- Be unclear about expectations and commitment. Set the bar low for both, but expect your group to grow in depth quickly. It should not take that much time to reach the protected soul.
- Keep people guessing by not creating a rhythm of meeting days and times. Avoid weekly meetings because people do not need to debrief and recalibrate their ongoing lives. Not enough life happens between meetings; it is just easier to "not bring things up"—to save ourselves the time to explain the backstories of such life situations and events. It is easier to just keep things to ourselves.
- Do not meet or communicate outside of these times through social media or meeting for coffee. Avoid having fun together. Avoid invitations to attend events together (such as ball games, movies, camping trips), as Christians are not allowed to enjoy life. Most people are too busy for these activities anyway.
- Be unprepared. Do not do any homework, but show your group how much you know while belittling them for their lack of biblical knowledge. Better yet, minimize the time spent in Bible study. Focus on the world, not the Word. There is more interesting subject matter to discuss, such as sports teams, culinary experiments, and vacation plans. Talk more and listen less. Hang out, do not hang tough.

- Avoid opportunities to genuinely care for one another. People want to be left alone to fend for themselves. Keep your honest thoughts to yourself. Other people cannot really help your situation.
- Share as few meals together as possible. These only provide for comfortable conversations and unnecessary debriefing of life stories.
- Assure people that they are the only ones who have a sin problem, or a sin problem as great as theirs. Remind them that only those who have their lives together will fit in and there is no room for struggles, shortcomings, conflicts, weaknesses, or doubts.
- Avoid sharing prayer concerns or praises. People are more interested in bringing their own needs before God, not the needs of others.
- Close your group to anyone else who would want to join, especially someone who would require investment and attention because they are new believers.
- Do not exercise any of the means of grace, such as prayer, Bible reading and study, worship, and silence and solitude, and definitely do not reflect on these together as a group.
- There is no need to celebrate small or large victories and life accomplishments. People do not want attention brought to themselves.
- Decline any opportunity to serve the larger community. Convince your group there are no real individual or corporate benefits in serving together.

Elements of this humorous approach to small group dynamics is sadly a reality in many groups. The quality of time spent with each other is vital. Each point above reduces opportunities for conference, and thus for a deeper community that lives the gospel.

SOUL-TO-SOUL PROMPTS

Informational

1. What are some various ways love is understood in the world? How would you define love?

2. Familiarize yourself with the A-C-T-S acrostic (Adoration, Confession, Thanksgiving, and Supplication [asking for things]) for prayer.

3. Make a list of what you know about Job from the book by the same name.

4. Whether streamed or in-person, what was the topic of last Sunday's sermon?

Transitional

1. The first use of the word "love" in the Bible is found in Genesis 22:2: "Take your son," he said, "your only son, Isaac, whom you love, to the land of Moriah, and offer him there as a burnt offering on one of the mountains I will tell you about." God establishes what love is: the willingness for the Father to sacrifice His Son and the willingness of the Son to be sacrificed. How does this definition compare with yours?

2. Individually, spend ten minutes praying A-C-T without the "S."

3. The book of Job demonstrates far more than the familiar idiom, "You have the patience of Job." It is about the sovereignty of a powerful and all-knowing God against the backdrop of suffering. From chapters 38 to 42, how does God describe His sovereignty?

4. What biblical truths were your takeaways? What was revealed about Jesus?

Transformational

1. If you have ever wrestled with knowing that God loves you, how might this perspective change your understanding and the implications of this gift of divine love?

2. Reconvene to share your reflections from your time praying A-C-T without the "S."
   ⊚ How often did supplication slip in?
   ⊚ What might be revealed about your relationship with God?

How did this prayer exercise show a greater emphasis on what we want God to give us versus adoring Him for who He is?

◉ How does one grow to know God better and thus adore Him more fully?

◉ God wants us to ask Him for things that are important in our lives, so supplication is necessary. Yet, how is the frequency, intensity, and worry of "supplicating" affected when you intentionally focus more on adoring God?

3. God essentially challenges you as He did Job, "Show them how it is done, (insert your name), when a righteous person suffers." What challenges, potential anxiety, or fears, inward and outward, are you facing in a current period of suffering? How does knowing He is sovereign in and over everything impact your situation? Be specific.

4. If this truth is deeply believed in your heart, how might it be manifested in your life? For what would you need to depend on God's Spirit to give you in evidence of His manifestation and rule? Be specific as you apply this to a present and particular life situation.

CHAPTER 7

FAMILY CONFERENCES OF
THE CONVERSATION KIND

*You are not like to see any general reformation, till
you procure family reformation.*

Richard Baxter, *Reformed Pastor*

*The greatest legacy one can pass on to one's children
and grandchildren is not money or other material
things accumulated in one's life, but rather a legacy
of character and faith.*

Billy Graham

SOUL-TO-SOUL PURPOSE

The family is the focus of many Puritan
writers. Puritans have referred to the
family as "a little church," "a seminary of
the Church and commonwealth," and a
"school of Christ." Indeed, every household
was regarded as a religious community.
William Gouge describes the family as "a
beehive, in which is the stock, and out of

||||||||||||||||||||||||||||||||||||||||||

HISTORICAL SNAPSHOT

William Gouge (1578–1653)
was an English clergyman,
prolific author, and skilled expositor. His admirers called him "the
father of the London Divines
and the oracle of his time." One
of his most famous works, *Of
Domesticall Duties*, provided an
analysis of the godly household.

which are sent many swarms of bees: for in families are all sorts of people bred and brought up: and out of families are they sent into the Church and common-wealth."[1] Healthy churches and a morally healthy society consist of individuals who were raised in spiritually and morally healthy families.

||||||||||||||||||||||||||||||||||||

HISTORICAL SNAPSHOT

William Perkins (1558–1602) indulged in recklessness, profanity, black magic, the occult, and drunkenness as a youth. His conversion experience while at Cambridge changed his personal life and led him to pursue theological studies. Perkins's *A garden of spirituall flowers* is one of the earliest Puritan devotional manuals.

||||||||||||||||||||||||||||||||||||

HISTORICAL SNAPSHOT

John Norton (1606–1663) was an English-born preacher who immigrated to America. His work, *Abel being Dead Yet Speaketh,* is credited with being the first biography written in America and presents a short history of the life of John Cotton.

A great responsibility for spiritual growth lies within the home. Parenting involves teaching children and others in the household the ways of God. Both sons and daughters are recipients of such godly counsel. William Perkins, a Puritan preacher and theologian, advises the family to "use meditation and conference about heavenly things; assemble thy family together, confer with them what they have learned at the sermon; instruct and catechize them, read, or cause to be read somewhat of the Bible, or some other godly book unto them."[2]

The responsibility for the welfare of the souls of children rests on parents. Puritans regarded fathers as pastors of their flocks and their attention was necessarily drawn to promoting family prayers, Bible study, teaching the children, and family church attendance. J. I. Packer sums, "The principle here is that the man of the house has an inalienable responsibility to care for the souls of the household, and that it is on the Lord's Day supremely that he must exercise it. The Puritan pastor, unlike his modern counterpart, did not scheme to reach the men through the women and children, but *vice versa*."[3] Puritan John Norton described fathers who paid greater attention to worldly gain than to the training of their children as those "who are very careful for the shoe, and take no care for the foot."[4]

The responsibility and privilege of conferencing with family members rests with the heads of households. Mothers and fathers teach and instruct their children, connecting scriptural truths from sermons and their own Bible reading.

SOUL-TO-SOUL PERSPECTIVE

In the books of the Law, God discloses that He is relational. He cares about His relationship with people and their relationships with each other. In Deuteronomy—meaning "second law"—Moses reminds the Israelites of God's holiness and love and His faithful work through their history. In response, God's people are to love Him with their whole being. Loving obedience should be the recognizable trait of believers. This principle was taught and lived out, as Deuteronomy 6:5–9 reveals.

> Love the LORD your God with all your heart, with all your soul, and with all your strength. These words that I am giving you today are to be in your heart. *Repeat* them to your children. Talk about them when you sit in your house and when you walk along the road, when you lie down and when you get up. Bind them as a sign on your *hand* and let them be a symbol on your *forehead*. Write them on the doorposts of your *house* and on your city *gates*. (Emphasis added)

The family is God's primary learning community. Being a parent is an essential and noble calling, as is the responsibility to deeply influence the next generation in a godly way. This relationship between parent and child works to form the child's brain and mind, which biblically is the heart.[5] The primary command to love precedes the stipulation to teach. Notice the realms where teaching is applied: *personal* (hands and foreheads), *family* (the doorposts of the home), and the *public arena* (the 'gate').

Teaching starts with one's own personal fidelity, your own faithfulness to God. Your words and actions reflect belief and devotion to the Lord. It begins with salvation, your relationship with Jesus as Lord and Savior. You have been removed from the kingdom of darkness and transferred into the kingdom of light. We do not enter God's kingdom because it will make all things better, or because our family members or our friends did, or because we live in a "Christian" nation. We believe God's "good news"—the gospel—because it is true. The gospel is "God with us," coming nearer and nearer throughout redemptive history until now He resides in us. God now inclines our hearts toward Him and toward His life-giving Word (1 Kings 8:58) and we join Him in pointing our children's hearts toward Him (Proverbs 4:20–27). Doubts arise when we place our faith in our faith, which wavers. Placing our faith in God, who is unchanging, reminds us of the anchoring truth of who He is.

Meditating on God's Word allows it to impact the heart deeply. Some Puritans referred to biblical meditation as conferencing with ourselves, where biblical knowledge converges with the state of our soul. Conferencing with ourselves can yield observable differences that serve to display God's character. Our lives show that God is real and that Jesus is who He says He is. Evidence of God working in the world today is proof of His Spirit manifested in and through believers.

The second realm where teaching is applied is in the home and family. Faith and allegiance to God are initially transmitted in the home, through the mundane ordinariness of life. We gain a strong sense of God's desire for the family in the way He desires to be addressed. He delights in being called Father, and He is the perfect parent to us. This impacts how we parent our children as their primary discipler for much of their formative years. For as many children with which one has been gifted, a parent must become a growing expert on each, catching glimpses of how God uniquely fashioned each child with a given personality, nature, temperament, and abilities. Parents must, from the start, seek to discover the ways God has wired their child through all stages of growth—infant, toddler, teenager, young adult, and everything in between. These truths inform us how to parent. Observe and get to know your child, not through the lens of who or what you want them to be but for the ways and purposes God made them. Discover how each best receives information, love, correction, and praise. And discover how they best hear and take matters to heart. Chances are, it will not be through raising your voice, incessantly repeating yourself (otherwise they would have heard you the first time), or threats. Hearing precedes speaking (Deuteronomy 31:12) and is the key to the heart.[6] Talk to your children about how you best hear something. Discover together how each child hears best. A "hearing heart" afforded Solomon great wisdom (1 Kings 3:9–12).

The third realm of impact for teaching is the public arena. Public teaching is about integrity, living life consistent with what you believe about God and the way He sees and values others. We are made to know and reflect Him wherever we are, whoever we are with, and whatever the time of day. The integration of faith and life observed in the home now extends outside the home. This could be the marketplace or the market, campus or campground, vocation or vacation. Frequent opportunities are given daily to authenticate that what you believe about God is true. It is expressed in your words and actions.

The impact of teaching in these three realms has a purpose: to avoid idolatry, the worship of creature or created instead of Creator. Deuteronomy 4 is replete with sustained commands to avoid idolatry, and it is no surprise to see the accompanying emphases on teaching. They are mutually effecting; being attentive to teaching prevents idolatry, and teaching aims to keep future generations from adopting idolatrous values.

Teaching in each of these three realms involves conferencing. Spiritual conversations that connect biblical truths with soul care foster learning, values, assurance, and transformation that are communicated and lived.

SOUL-TO-SOUL PARTICIPANTS

Though not a Puritan herself, Susanna Wesley, mother to Charles and John Wesley, grew up in a Puritan home. Her father, Samuel Annesley, was a Nonconformist minister who helped facilitate the Puritan movement alongside notable contemporaries Richard Baxter and John Owen. Wesley was highly educated, and in marriage followed her husband into the rustic setting of the Lincolnshire parishes, but did not abandon her conscience

HISTORICAL SNAPSHOT

Susanna Wesley (1669–1742) had a family heritage that was strongly Puritan. At a young age, however, Wesley chose to separate from Nonconformist ranks and join the established Church of England. Sons Charles and John were cofounders of the Methodist movement.

nurtured in Puritan London. Of the eighteen or nineteen children to whom she gave birth, only ten survived. She may have taken to heart the words of Timothy Rogers, as he spoke these words at her sister Elizabeth's funeral: "Mothers may do great service to religion, by leaving good advice to their children." In developing this point, he stated:

> If good women would apply themselves to reading and study, as the men do, or had equal advantage for knowledge in their education, no doubt we should have more of their excellent composures, many of them have a happy genius, and a smooth expression, and might write as well as work, and the pen might have as good success as the needle; especially, they may make observations, or draw up rules for the good order of their own families, and when they see fit, communicate them for the good of others.[7]

When each child turned five, a discipline in Wesley's parenting practice was a household schedule initiated with a daylong first reading lesson, using the book of Genesis as a primer. She believed in the education of her children—daughters as well as sons. In a letter written to her son on the education of children, she asserted:

> That no girl be taught to work till she can read very well . . . for the putting children to learn sewing before they can read perfectly is the very reason why so few women can read fit to be heard, and never to be well understood.[8]

As her children grew, she devoted a weekly conference to each one. She used this time for personal instruction in the faith, incorporating a variety of age-appropriate spiritual activities. Her pedagogical skills affirmed the importance she gave to the theological training of her children. Wesley's dedication to her children's education and the format she employed was notable. Her use of conference was clear.

John Wesley incorporated conference into the use of his small groups called "classes" and "bands." These meetings were designed to nurture the spiritual growth of his followers through fellowship and accountability.

He found conference as an effective means for mutual encouragement and growth in faith and holiness. It is interesting to note that these meetings were scheduled for Thursdays, the same day his mother held weekly conferences with him as a young child. How impacting early childhood spiritual training can be!

SOUL-TO-SOUL PERKS

There is great satisfaction in knowing that our children invest in closer and continued walks with God. We desire this for our children not only because it benefits them the most and most effectively avoids dangerous pitfalls, but because we long for them to be independent adults dependent on God. We desire that their identity and security be found in Him and that they realize they are of cosmic significance because they are made in the image of God. This is a worthy vision for our children.

God establishes a principle of casting a vision for His people. He gives a vision of the future to His people through the promise and consistent descriptions of the Promised Land, the coming Messiah, the new heavens and new earth, and His fulfilled coming kingdom. These truths impact His people's response, how they choose to live in the present.

Parents too can cast a vision for each of their children. Conferences with our children support the unique God-ordained vision for their lives. As growing experts of our children, parents can take God-given insights and observations to communicate strengths and weaknesses in age-appropriate ways that focus more on the heart or motivation of a behavior than on the act itself. This better equips parents for helpful conversations on tough matters.

My friend Elijah needed to have a tough conversation with his high-school-aged son and wanted to cast a vision for his future. He reminded his firstborn of the lifelong family values of growing in character, of being self-sufficient, and of being a godly man. Part of the conversation revolved around success as seen through the eyes of God, the gaining of understanding and wisdom by deeply absorbing and assimilating God's Word. The conversation built on positive attributes and strengths in his son observed and confirmed over the years. This was particularly impacting as this teenager was able to list, almost too easily, his numerous weaknesses, yet could not come up with strengths.

To learn from failures and that the process is more important than the outcome is difficult to hear, even from a supportive dad. Yet the consistent encouragement of hearing his father's (and mother's) assurance of being available for his son was life-affirming. It was the safety net that instilled greater confidence in this young man, so much so that his countenance and actions soon afterward reflected an increased self-assurance.

Through this and other conversations, Elijah asked himself if it was his own pride that often pushed his children and prevented him taking the more time-involved approach of determining what each child needed in a given moment and stage in life. It is important to remember that the way parents parent will impact how their children will parent their own children one day. This is a crucial vision for parents.

SOUL-TO-SOUL PAUCITY

In a 2016 report titled "Top 10 Findings on Teens and the Bible," Barna Group found that 47 percent of the surveyed teens strongly agree that the Bible is a source of hope. About a third of teens believe the Bible contains everything a person needs to know to live a meaningful life. These figures were significantly higher for teens who are practicing Protestants. David Kinnaman, president of Barna Group and director of the study, states the research "tells us that teens have a deep respect for the Bible and care about its relevance to the world in which they inhabit."[9] Add these encouraging research findings to some sobering ones from the same year.

In a recent report from the CIRP Freshman Survey 2016, researchers noted a significant percentage of students who felt anxious or depressed or overwhelmed by all they had to do. Many anticipated seeking professional counseling. They were generally eager to get involved on campus and to share their views, but also wanted support to navigate their new environment.[10] The results of this study were important enough to suggest that colleges need to be prepared to address mental health concerns of incoming students.

The need for consistent and intentional connections between parents and their children is greater now than ever before. A disconnect in a relationship with parents can cause a disconnect with a child's faith. Though teenagers may think it is "cool" to ignore, distance oneself from, or criticize parents, it can be hurtful to be the object of these actions from your child. They still, however, need you. Be courageous in initiating conference with your child. Be the kind of parent who seeks and keeps seeking to understand their heart and soul, while staying sensitive to the way they receive your gestures. Be the kind of parent they want to talk with and one they know will listen. Extend and express, with unwavering commitment, the forgiveness, love, and grace needed to help them navigate shifting waters. And while you are at it, consider how you are a living expression of this to your teen's circle of friends.

SOUL-TO-SOUL PREPARATION

Getting to know God more deeply is the best way to grow your relationship with your children. As you observe how God is Father to His people, you may come across implications that impact your parenting. Notice also the presence Jesus extended toward those with whom He engaged in conversation. His nearness, touch, voice, and integrity encourage us to do the same.

Current research highlights the need for real conversation. Sherry Turkle observes that we have moved from speaking through our machines to speaking to them. Her pro-conversation but not necessarily anti-technology approach is helpful for grasping what technology is doing to our conversations, and thus to us. Even the presence of a silent phone changes what people talk about. Fragmented conversations have compromised our relationships, creativity, and ability to empathize.[11]

Here are some practical ways to cultivate healthy conversations aimed at connecting with your children:

- Avoid succumbing to "distracted parenting." Turn off your devices and televisions; stay tuned to your child. Get to know them for who they are and are becoming. Social media turns everything into "breaking news" and keeps the mind "on alert," while fueling the fear of missing out (FOMO) in them and in us. This takes a toll on the soul. To counter the addictive draw of how many "likes" or comments one receives on a post, communicate affirmation and validation of your child's personal worth through your voice, which echoes God's.

- Counter the busyness of distracted living. Set up device-free parts of your home and device-free times, such as meals together. Engage your children with meaningful conversations. Share at least one meal each day together where mutual and meaningful conversations take place. Your children really do want to share these meals with you.

- Do not assume you know what they are thinking and why. Ask well-framed questions suited to the way they best receive inquiries. Refrain from thinking and answering for them; consider how to get them to think out loud. Be patient, listening and watching as they process and offer their own answers.

- Do not minimize their difficulties. Affirm the reality of these challenges, but do not get so tangled in the present that you lose sight of the future; cast a vision of God's presence, direction, and purpose.

- Be aware of the idols of entitlement, materialism, autonomy, relativism, and individualism; represent God's kingdom as the pre-ferred option. Be prepared to tell them why. We all make mistakes; ask for forgiveness. Model what asking for forgiveness and living out forgivenness looks like.

- Avoid the threat of being "just Christian enough"; children deserve to see "all-in" lives of integrity.

- Avoid filling the calendar with too many extra-curricular activi-ties for your child; these may augment character development, but are not substitutes for a parent's touch and personal investment in each child. Try to build in times of silence and solitude for your child.

SOUL-TO-SOUL PROMPTS

Here are some overarching postures that fuel each of the subsequent groups of prompts.

Regularly talk with and pray for your children. Talk about what you are learning about God through His Word or a sermon. Take advantage of the captive audience you have during car rides without radio background noise. Model interest and delight in conversing with your children, taking advantage of teachable moments.

Your children are watching you read God's Word and they know when you have spent time with Him or not. Avoid using a Bible app on your device. It is difficult to tell the difference between playing a game, watching a film, or reading from your Bible app. Develop a rhythm of meeting God through His Word. Allow the truths from God's Word to sink more deeply into your heart.

Cultivate having the mind of Christ. Talk about the wrestling in coming to ultimately follow Him and why that was an important moment in your life. Tell stories of His faithfulness and your obedience. Reflecting on His majesty, power, and intimate involvement in your life promotes humility and thankfulness in you and your young listener. As you grow increasingly familiar with being present before God and with your children, you will be better able to connect who your child is becoming with how God made them to be.

YOUNG CHILDREN

For young children, keep discovering how God wired them. Take note of their natural talents and interests and how they like to be recognized and thanked. Notice their propensity toward introversion and extroversion, knowing that each of these has powerful and impacting strengths. Show them what unconditional love looks and sounds like. Point out ways they can begin to see the kindnesses of God. These can be applied to grandchildren too.

Informational

1. Where's the moon? Add comments to the answer.

2. Read, sing, draw, or imagine aspects of creation.

3. Which friends did you see at church today?

4. Identify body parts as a game or song.

5. What made today a good (or bad) day?

6. Read Psalm 19 or Psalm 104.

7. Are you little? Is Jesus big?

8. Let's spend some time just being quiet together.

Transitional

1. Who made the moon? Add your affirmation of God having made the moon.

2. Convey truths about Creation as you draw or observe nature.

3. Which Bible story character did you hear about today?

4. Who made each of those parts?

5. God was right there with you in your good (or bad) day.

6. What comes to mind when you think of what God does?

7. If Jesus lives in you, He must be showing!

8. What are you thinking about?

Transformational

1. Repeat these questions with other features of creation.

2. Affirm God's goodness in all He created.

3. What did this person know about God and how did that show up in his/her actions?

4. Identify parts of the body that cannot be seen. Affirm that God made those as well.

5. What do you think God thought about what happened today?

6. Pray and thank God for who He is and what He has done.

7. How is Jesus showing in you to others?

8. I appreciate the quiet times with you and the thoughts you have. Whether we are together or not, these times are good for you and me.

PRETEEN

In the garden of Eden, God said yes to everything for Adam and Eve except the tree of knowledge. Explain that being a "Yes" parent means that there will be great freedom in what is allowed as long as it honors God and does no harm to self or others. In other words, when the answer is "No," that means no, but every "No" answer comes with a reasonable and clear explanation of why. The child can expect pushback if and when challenged. It will be particularly important to grow in sensitivity to God's Spirit as He directs your attitude and words, whether to speak or not. Your preteen will be given opportunities to authenticate their new creation self (2 Corinthians 5:17). Their life-giving decisions will require your prayer intervention. Parents battle for their children most effectively on their knees in prayer.

Informational

1. What made this day incredible? A challenge?

2. What movie did you and your friends see at the theater (or on Netflix)?

3. Read Psalm 13.

4. Because you are in Christ, by the grace of God, you belong to Him (1 Corinthians 6:19-20).

5. Who would you consider your good friends? Why?

6. Where is your favorite place to spend a few minutes alone with your thoughts?

Transitional

1. What might God be doing in this situation?

2. Was it a thumbs-up or thumbs-down film? Who would you recommend to see (or not see) this movie?

3. Have you ever felt the way this psalmist describes? Where is God in these moments?

4. What does it feel like to belong? How do people behave when they do not think they belong?

5. How do your friends reflect Jesus? How do they not reflect Jesus?

6. Would you share that place with me, though not necessarily together?

Transformational

1. How might God's desires impact your prayers for this situation?

2. How did it make you feel? What kinds of emotions were stirred up?

3. Why do you think God cares about our emotions? What might God be doing when He appears to be silent or absent?

4. To whom has God brought your attention to extend friendship?

5. How do your friends encourage you to follow Jesus? How do they present a challenge for you to follow Jesus?

6. What is it like to be in that place? What kinds of thoughts come to mind when you are there?

TEENAGERS

Some of the best times in my parenting years came when all four of our children were teenagers. It was not always easy, but it was remarkable to see their growth in making decisions, to be with them when suffering consequences of poor ones, and to enjoy their growth in becoming responsible, respectful, Jesus-centered, others-focused young pre-adults. Children of physically, mentally, or emotionally absent parents often feel misunderstood or not heard. Over time and with repeated nonengagement, many teens will seek being understood and heard from others, who cannot offer the counsel you are equipped to give.

Many of the challenges in these growing years come in the form of insecurity, founded on the fear of rejection or failure. Parents can identify and resonate with those fears and help draw their teenage child out. They, and we, need to be reminded that fear is looking into the future without God in it.

Informational

1. Consider this: *Shalom* is the life experience of the peace of well-being.

2. Because you are in Christ, by the grace of God, you are complete in Him. What does this mean?

3. What's your favorite book of the Bible? What makes it your favorite? From which part of God's Word are you reading and thinking about now?

4. If you are interested in someone, read 1 Corinthians 13:4–7.

5. What does this phrase mean? "You are not defined by your sin."

6. How would you describe forgiveness?

7. What are some of the fears your friends have talked about?

8. Some teenagers see being online as a time spent in silence. How do you understand being silent?

Transitional

1. What gets in the way of you experiencing *shalom*?

2. What are some ways you observe how friends or acquaintances seek to be complete?

3. What is God revealing about Himself as you read His Word?

4. Substitute that person's name wherever you see the word love in these four verses. Now substitute your name in those places.

5. If sin does not define a person, what does?

6. What benefits are there in forgiving someone? What harm is there in not forgiving?

7. Do you resonate with any of these fears? What is it like to be fearful?

8. Where do you like to go to be alone with your thoughts? Outside, in nature? Inside, in a favorite quiet spot?

Transformational

1. Praying for *shalom* for yourself and for others can be difficult. How will you depend on God's Spirit to do this?

2. How does knowing you are complete in Christ affect your view of yourself?

3. How is God proving to you that He is who He says He is in His Word? What observable difference do you see of that truth?

4. How well did this person, and you, pass the 1 Corinthians 13 test? (See Appendix 1)

5. In Christ you are completely forgiven. This truth allows you to walk into who God created you to be. Sin does not define you, God does. What is He saying about you?

6. Jesus provides a way for each of us to be forgiven, and one of the responses to this gift is to forgive others. If you consider the

human body, all the body parts are designed to move forward. Forgiveness allows us to move forward. How is God wanting you to move forward by extending forgiveness to a particular person?

7. A familiar command in Scripture is "Fear not." What attribute of God, if adopted in your heart, would cause you to trust Him more and to "fear not"?

8. How would you describe the quiet in nature to your friends? What benefits did you experience?

ADULT CHILDREN

The most nerve-racking text message I ever sent to my adult children regarding their growth in Christlikeness was, "Would you tell me what I did right and not so right?" I hesitated in sending the text, second-guessing it, tempted to delete it and move on with my life. Yet that was nothing compared to their lack of any response to the text. You can imagine the thoughts swirling in the back of my mind when no response was immediately received. But, as usual, there were good reasons for the delay. They were able to respond to my question around the dinner table at a restaurant four (long) days later. A couple shared comments deeply touched my heart. Hearing "You were always there" and "You had a unique approach toward each of us" was humbling. Though these reflections were of the past, opportunities continue to present themselves to shape them.

After a breakfast together, and having been convicted by God's Spirit of some words I had spoken, I texted an adult child to apologize for the prideful self-centeredness of my words. Though God continues to discipline me, I am hopeful that I will model for my children sensitivity to His Spirit, Christlike humility, dying to self, courage to follow through, and seeking forgiveness.

Whenever possible, I conference with our children (including our son-in-love), just to do a life and heart check. We chat about their walks with God, the God-given challenges they face, and the thoughts and actions that the Spirit may be leading them into and through. They are encouraged by the challenge of living *coram Deo*, living in the presence and under the authority of God to the glory of God. Many opportunities present themselves to reduce the tendency for pretense, to encourage, and to be fully present with my young adults. Our meetings cause me to think of and pray for them even more frequently and specifically.

My son-in-love Sean reflects on our meetings together:

> In our time together, you made it clear to me that you were meeting with all of your children for the same kind of interaction. This made me feel accepted as one of your own. While enjoying dim sum, we discussed how my walk with God was going, where I saw him working in my life. To be honest, at first I had no answer. Not because God wasn't there, but because I hadn't been sincerely looking. This taught me that I need to not just assume, but assess what He is doing. (I find it easier to see when looking back after the fact.) So, I looked at my life, at work and at home, and started to see where I should be present and where I should pray. This has helped me progress as the time goes by, because I can see tougher times as opportunities to pray or be present, which makes me feel more purposeful and less likely to become overwhelmed. Looking back, I would say, God has been working on me through these meetings. And I am blessed to have the time with you.

TWO NOTES TO PARENTS

1. It is not unusual for parents to wish they knew more about God the Father, Jesus the Son, the Holy Spirit, and the Bible. A common reaction is to relinquish the input and influence on a child's spiritual growth to the church. The quantity and quality of opportunities afforded by parents in the home, however, cannot begin to compare to the one or two hours spent once a week in a church setting. Search for answers to your questions from those in the church. They will welcome your inquiries and will help guide you to useful resources.

2. This note is for those parents experiencing the heartache of an adult prodigal child. The loving thoughts are many and the opportunities

for conversations may be few. The apostle Paul reminds his readers that God's kindness leads to repentance (Romans 2:4). In His kindness He ordained you to be a parent. You need to know that of all the people in the world, He chose you to be the parent of this child, knowing that there is no one else like you to persist in the commitment to love and pray for this child. Lean harder into God who is and continues to be kind to you and to your child. When you are given an opportunity, however brief it may be, try to speak these simple words: "God is kind to you." These few and unpretentious words are truth, and the timely repetition of them can find their way into a hearing and accepting heart that was once hard and unreceptive. God can use His and your words to remind a prodigal that the kindness of God is seen in the most challenging of situations and times. Be vigilant in conference with a trusted friend who knows your heart, assures you of God's sustaining presence and work, and supports you in prayer.

TWO NOTES TO TEENAGERS:

1. Give yourself time to learn about God. You do not have to know everything by the age of ten. Ask Bible questions of your parents or other older trusted adults. They would consider it an honor to help you grow closer to God.

2. If you are a teenager and having these types of conversations seems foreign to you or uncharacteristic of the relationship you have with your parent(s), then you may be the one called to step up. Consider being the one who initiates meaningful conversations with your parent(s). God may use you to grow and bless your family. Here's a start.

Informational

1. What about our family brings a smile to your face?

2. How was your day at work (or job-hunting) today?

3. How are you really feeling today? What's on your mind?

4. Why do you go to church?

5. Why do you read the Bible?

6. What part of the Bible are you reading now?

Transitional

1. A smile comes to my face when I think this about our family:

_____

2. What is the most difficult part of your work? What is most rewarding?

3. Offer a word of empathy.

4. What do you enjoy most about church? Why?

5. How often do you get to read it?

6. What are you learning about Jesus?

Transformational

1. God has been kind to our family. Briefly explain what you see. Express thankfulness.

2. How can I be keeping you in prayer over a specific work situation?

3. What specific prayer concern may I bring before God?

4. How are you changed by going to church?

5. What difference do you see in yourself after you spend time with God in the Bible?

6. In what ways do you depend on God's Spirit to become more like Jesus?

CHAPTER 8

MARRIAGE CONFERENCES OF
THE CONVERSATION KIND

To love at all is to be vulnerable.

C. S. Lewis, *Four Loves*

Watch over the hearts and lives of one another, and labor to discern the state of one another's souls and the strength or weakness of each other's sins and graces and the failings of each other's lives, so that you may be able to apply to one another the most suitable help.

Richard Baxter, *Godly Home*

SOUL-TO-SOUL PURPOSE

It would be easy to think the Puritans were prudish when it comes to matters of marriage. This stereotype has persisted, even as longstanding scholarship and the Puritans' own writings prove otherwise. The Puritans understood the impact marriage and family life had on society.

With the Bible as its primary source, conference between spouses is an exchanged gift of time and words. Husbands and wives discuss spiritual matters and issues on an equal basis with each other. Creating the emotional environment conducive to revealing one's and one another's needs fosters caring for each other's souls. This is a responsibility not lightly taken, as Richard Baxter describes:

> Do not conceal the state of your souls or hide your faults from one another. You are as one flesh and should have one heart. As it is dangerous for a man not to know his own needs, so it is hurtful for a husband or wife not to know the other's needs.[1]

Puritans applied this practically in their marriage relationships.

Puritan Nehemiah Wallington, a lathe worker, reflects on two of the many times in his three decades of marriage when he wrestled with matters of his faith. His apparent failure to pray as he had intended brought on worrisome thoughts. Prayer in his closet was then followed by "much sweetness & profit in reading and praying with my family: and these meditations & conference I had with my wife, I had in residue of the day."[2] On a separate occasion, Wallington reflects on the events of his day as he pens, ". . . upon examination I find that I spent two hours in the morning in speech with my wife, some of the world, some of heaven, and how I may glorify God."[3]

|||||||||||||||||||||||||||||||||||||||

HISTORICAL SNAPSHOT

Nehemiah Wallington (1598–1658) was a turner (or lathe worker) and diarist. A rare glimpse of life through the eyes of a typical London Puritan artisan has been preserved through more than 2,600 pages of personal papers and works—memoirs, religious reflections, sermon notes, political reportage, letters, and a spiritual diary.

Helping to further each other's growth in godliness involves "frequent discussions about such things as concerned growing in grace, mutually asking questions to one another, and answering them."[4] This practice and example modeled patterns of godliness for each other.

SOUL-TO-SOUL PERSPECTIVE

Marriage matters. Your marriage matters. From their research on the American family, a diverse team of leading family scholars presented three fundamental conclusions: 1. The intact biological, married family remains the gold standard for family life in the United States. 2. Marriage is an important public good. 3. The benefits of marriage extend to poor, working class, and minority communities.[5] They also found these benefits:

- Marriage increases the likelihood that fathers and mothers have good relationships with their children.
- Marriage, and a normative commitment to marriage, fosters high-quality relationships between adults, as well as between parents and children.
- Married couples seem to build more wealth on average than singles or cohabiting couples.
- Married men earn more money that do single men with similar education and job histories.
- Married people, especially married men, have longer life expectancies than do otherwise similar singles.
- Marriage is associated with better health and lower rates of injury, illness, and disability for both men and women.
- Children whose parents divorce have higher rates of psychological distress and mental illness.
- Married mothers have lower rates of depression than do single or cohabiting mothers.
- Marriage appears to reduce the risk that adults will be either perpetrators or victims of crime.
- A child who is not living with his or her own two married parents is at a greater risk of child abuse.

Marriage will not solve all social and cultural problems, nor are all marriages equal, but marriage does matter, and it matters more than and beyond the consequences of social and public good.

Consideration of marriage must include God's divine perspective and purpose. Marriage was designed to be more than a private, mutually satisfying, enthusiastically emotional, family-creating relationship. God created and designed marriage to model His love for humans and His church. Marriages are to be living witnesses to His faithfulness and commitment, with the goal of reflecting Him to a scrutinizing world. It is called image-bearing. God engages with each life partner to grow their character and to share His love. This God-initiated love, revealed and extended to each other, is then to impact and influence the couple's world and the world around them. God's unconditional love is the most vital expression of His character in a Christ follower. Because God is holy and because love comes from God, holiness will be a critical component of our expressions of love.

Gary Thomas asks, "What if God designed marriage to make us holy more than to make us happy?"[6] Happiness used to be a virtue; now it is a goal. Holiness, though, is commanded by God in both the Old Testament and the New Testament. God says to Moses, "Speak to the entire Israelite community and tell them: Be holy, because I, the LORD your God, am holy" (Leviticus 19:2). As God's representatives on earth, we are living stories meant to showcase the characteristics that are similar to God's. The words of Peter to believers amid great suffering and persecution, "But as the one who called you is holy, you also are to be holy in all your conduct; for it is written, Be holy, because I am holy" (1 Peter 1:15–16), was a charge to live distinctively. God is the standard for how we conduct our lives. The Greek word for holy is *hagios* and the root meaning of *hagios* is "different." The Christ follower is different from others. In belonging to God, one's life reflects the purity and love of God. This is the calling to be different, that by His Spirit, we live out our pedigree.

Perhaps this is why the Puritans called their spiritual conversations *Holy* Conference.

The difference-making conversations in your marriage matter to your spouse and to God. Communication in marriage is necessary. Good communication in marriage is learned. Transforming communication in marriage is God's intent.

SOUL-TO-SOUL PARTICIPANTS

When the Bible says, the two shall become one flesh, it does not mean one person gets erased of opinions, needs, hopes, and dreams. When we say, "I do," we are agreeing with God as we enter a covenant relationship. God's covenant relationship with us—a relationship of lover and loved one—parallels the marriage relationship. The covenant relationship we have with our spouse is a sustained decision of faithfulness and permanence, based not on emotions but on commitment.

Books and conferences on marriage and communication in marriage are critical helps to grow and strengthen the bond between husbands and wives. When wedding vows are exchanged and each is given a title, husband or wife, we are not aware of all that these titles—and roles—entail. At this point, we do not know all there is to know about being a husband or a wife, but these titles mean that we are in the process of learning. The rest of our committed life together becomes the lab practicum of learning and living out what it means to be married.

The knitting together of each other's spirits comes as each spouse shares from a deep well of needs and desires. This guides a couple to engage in nurturing their relationship, grounded in deepening trust and love. The most intimate kind of sharing can take place only when there is no fear of rejection. Being loving may have less to do with "being in love" and more to do with the intentionality of cultivating a relationship of respect, compassion, and acknowledgment.

Communications professor Tim Muehlhoff highlights what experts observe about the relational climate of our conversations: the manner in which we speak and act toward one another—with acknowledgment, expectations, trust, and commitment—impacts a conversation more than the content of what we say.[7]

SOUL-TO-SOUL PERKS

When our conversations are received well, personal insights about each other's life and world develop and a growing and deepening trust is built. And when our spiritual conversations are received well, the advancing of each other's growth in grace is furthered. Shared and exchanged thoughts, desires, hopes, dreams, and concerns strengthen the honor, regard, respect, and each other's reputations in a marriage.

Because God is always working to grow and mature us, the spiritual sensitivity and attentiveness that conference helps facilitate is heightened.

Spouses are better able to notice God, how He is working in each life and in them as a couple, and thus discover more about God Himself. This sensitivity includes partnering in affirming and reminding each other of your identity in Christ, being able to see and sense early warning signs of sin, and experiencing greater integrity in faith and behavior.

Taking opportunities to speak into each other to inform and remind ourselves of our identity in Christ combats the incessant barrage of advertisements, commercials, trailers, pop-ups, and billboards on television, the internet, our devices, and even in self-talk that undermines the truth of our being complete, forgiven, freed, alive, not condemned, rescued, loved, and given purpose in Christ. Knowing and living out our identity in Christ establishes a freedom to treat another person as one who is free to be who they are.[8] Your identity is not dependent on others but is with and from God, which enables the giving and receiving of help without fear of losing yourself. Opportunities to authenticate our new creation self contribute to a healthier relationship both in and outside our marriages.

The breadth and depth of knowing each other in marriage provides a unique posture from which to observe our lives with an alertness toward sin or actions that reveal disconnectedness from a heart that pleases God. These observations may be evidence of the subtle warfare aimed at derailing your marriage. Carefully and prayerfully guided words couched in grace-filled, truth-reflecting, and life-giving correction are born from the knowledge gained of each other's spiritual makeup and disposition. These words given and received are evidence of a mutual commitment to soul care and formation.

Matters discussed in conference prompt the formation of godly character, which yields greater integrity in faith and behavior. Individuals exhibit being the same person regardless of where they are, who they are with, and the time of day. Challenges are better navigated, victories are more frequently celebrated, and the commonplace matters of the day are seen as opportunities to grow gratefulness.

Not only do these advantages increase the attractiveness of one to the other, but the marriage becomes what God intended. He delights in marriages that serve as a witness of dependence on His Spirit to nurture and mature this most intimate of relationships and to reveal its meaning and purpose to each spouse and the observing world.

SOUL-TO-SOUL PAUCITY

The lack of good communication and, in particular, intentional conversations that connect one to another on a spiritual level is evidenced in many ways between marriage partners.

A lack of desire to know more deeply the one to whom a commitment for life was made increases the potential for increased secrecy and unresolved conflict. This unnecessarily burdens a couple beyond the expected challenges of two imperfect people in marital union. Decreased desire can be caused or complicated by the busyness that consumes our schedules. When sideswiped by the clamor of the urgent and the unrelenting demands of the insatiable self, couples can find themselves at a loss for time and attention needed to invest in one another and their marriage.

In some cases, indifference grows. This popular phrase is widely accepted by psychologists and sociologists: "The opposite of love is not hate, but indifference." No longer is there a need to extend respect, acknowledgment, or compassion. Indifference can manifest itself in disapproval, a disregard for input, icy distance, or prideful smugness.

Barbara Myerhoff is a sociologist who studied neglected patients in an elderly housing project in southern California. No one visited these elderly patients. She states that "unless we exist in the eyes of others, we may come to doubt even our own existence."[9] Apply this observation to communication dynamics in a marriage.

Baxter observed, "When either husband or wife is speaking seriously about holy things, let the other be careful to cherish and not to extinguish and put an end to the discourse."[10] The constant silence of the hearer and impertinent worldly talk are two ways that derail a conversation, sufficiently distancing it from heart and heaven. The sustained implied indifference complicates relationships and may bring one to question one's own purpose, being, or existence.

Other evidence of a dearth of spiritual conversations is lack of growth in knowing the Word and the God of the Word. Without a biblical blueprint for marriage, the big picture of the design, purpose, and means for a God-reflecting union is lost. Absence of the application of biblical truths within the sphere of committed marriage, which extends outwardly, weakens our testimony of a faithful God who is present, powerful, and forgiving. Conversations and the results of conversations are meant to bear witness to God's design for marriage. Without it, our imaging of His design for marriage and the Christlikeness that characterizes a believer in his or her relationships, for the sake of God and the world, will be deficient.

SOUL-TO-SOUL PREPARATION

Effective conference in any context requires ongoing preparation and reflection. In the marriage context, a mutuality of preparation is most helpful. Here are four aspects that help in the initiation and continuance of conference for husbands and wives.

First, learning to be present is quickly becoming a lost art. Competition for our time, attention, and affections is growing. Distracted living has become the norm and it is sabotaging our ability to communicate. We zone in and out of conversations, lacking the ability to be fully present with others and with God. William Gouge warned almost four hundred years ago of "[a] careless neglect . . . when husbands and wives are so attentive to earthly things that they think it enough if they provide one another with the things of this life."[11]

We have adopted distraction as an accepted mode of being. We have become addicted to distraction. Author Tony Reinke warns of psychological, physical, and spiritual consequences of digital distractions—they make us prone to depression and anxiety, less able to concentrate at work and to sleep at night.[12] Distraction in its many forms competes for and often wins the prize of our soul's attention, which is designed to find its fulfillment and contentment in experiencing the intimate presence of the Father, the life-transforming grace of Jesus, and the enabling power of the Holy Spirit.

Being in silence and solitude before God for even fifteen minutes can reveal not only the nature of an addiction to distractions but also the matters that disrupt our thoughts and conversations. Try this exercise a few times in a week. It will be uncomfortable initially for many of us, but do not be surprised if after just a couple attempts, you find a willingness to stay longer than fifteen minutes and to return to this again. It is God's way of saying, "Welcome. I have something for you." Growing more comfortable and familiar with being present before God affects our ability to be present with others, and this affects the needed skill to listen and understand them.

Second, being understood is one of the most powerful tools in any relationship and is especially important in the marriage relationship. Listening to understand is that keen ability to attend to someone in conversation in a manner that purposes to comprehend and empathize with their emotions.

Dr. John Gottman, a leading marriage researcher, found that emotionally intelligent couples demonstrate a genuine interest in the other's life and inner world, and as this knowledge grows, so does the relationship.[13] To gain a sense of the other's hopes, fears, dreams, worries, and goals requires listening to understand.

Muehlhoff identifies seven elements of listening to understand. The more any number of these elements appears in a conversation, the greater the probability that deeper understanding will occur.

- Desire to understand: This desire manifests in giving another the space to share thoughts without threat of interruption, evaluation, and pressure of time.
- Clarifying questions: The goal in asking questions is to further understand the message being conveyed.
- Summary statements: Paraphrasing by the listener can powerfully confirm the content and tone of the speaker's words.
- Perspective taking: Having set aside one's own views, this listening attempts to understand how the other views reality and how it feels to hold those beliefs.
- Mindfulness: This is the ability to be fully present before another, eliminating external distractions and internal diversions.
- Poetic moment: Detecting the moment when a person's heartfelt convictions offers a glimpse of their soul.[14]

Listening to understand requires a healthy and mature dose of Christlike humility. Whenever one prefers to rush in with answers, cut to the solution, make a premature judgment, or ignore the other, listening to understand requires denying the self. This form of denying is not acting out of false humility or sliding down a scale toward low self-worth. Instead, the interdependency cultivated by putting another before oneself sparks the transforming and redeeming aspects of God-purposed marriage. This then enhances, strengthens, and increases the grace and stamina needed to navigate well the inevitable challenges of a lifetime together.

Third, consider your speech. What and how you communicate matters to each other. Baxter's words highlight the depth of shared thoughts and conversations in the marriage relationship: "When you lie down and rise together, do not let your worldly business have all your talk, but let God and your souls have the first and the last and the freest and sweetest of your speech, if not the most."[15]

Gracious speech is associated with godly wisdom. Conversations that include validation and gratitude reflect spiritual maturity. Acknowledge difficulties and challenges in conversations. This builds empathy and can be done without solving a problem or minimizing the feelings associated with it. And be grateful. Saying "thank you" is humbling. It is recognizing that something was done that would not or could not have been done without the other. Without expressing thanksgiving, our gratitude is incomplete. Being thankful opposes the self, reduces the anxiety of receiving, fosters spiritual growth, particularly humility, and deepens trust.

Trust is one of the virtues and pillars of a successful marriage. Do not take it for granted. Vulnerability builds trust and, in an almost circular fashion, trust affords greater vulnerability. It must start somewhere with someone. Vulnerability is risky, but worth it. It also has an additional effect of mirroring the vulnerability and trust one develops before and with God.

Fourth, no one expects married couples to know it all, so seek help from others. Pursue reputable and godly counsel available through blogs, marriage conferences, books, and videos. For added engagement and benefit, consider doing any of the above with other like-hearted couples and friends.

To discover the thoughts, motivations, and workings of the whole person, which is the soul, and to communicate your understanding of these takes time and the gift of being present. The Spirit-guided attitude, manner, and words that give rise to your conversations honor your spouse and God. Conference makes us more aware of God's presence and more dependent on what He may be saying and doing.

SOUL-TO-SOUL PROMPTS

Informational

1. How is that group project you have been tackling at work?

2. I am grateful for these three things: _____ _____ _____.

3. What do you know about finding your identity in Christ? Many people are at a loss when faced with this question, but exploring this has a major impact on your soul and your relationships.

4. One of the indicators found in successful marriages is the ability to forgive. Forgiveness is not sweeping an issue under the rug or ignoring an injustice. Nor is it to be used as leverage, a tool for negotiating or manipulating, to prematurely end a discussion with an attitude of now not needing to talk about it again, or as a panacea to simply move on. Forgiveness is a gift that has been freely given, and once received is expected to be freely given—no required conditions or strings attached. This requires God-granted courage and effort, grace, and enabling because we do not have it in us to accomplish it in the manner He desires.

   Who are those who are easy to forgive? Not so easy to forgive? Impossible to forgive? Who is God presenting you with for whom you are reminded of the complete forgiveness you have already received and now are to extend to another? Your action is in obedience to God. That's what counts. The other person's response, or lack of, is not your responsibility. Your obedience is.

5. The word used to describe Satan's tactics in Genesis 3:1 is "cunning" or "crafty." His intent was to deceive and his approach sly. The serpent, in his cunningness or craftiness, uses just enough of God's truth and word to mislead and distort God's design. In what ways have you seen a distortion of God's design in the world?

Transitional

1. What is one challenge working with or leading this group?

2. Spouses are especially impacted by the words "Thank you." Complete this sentence and express this to your spouse. I am grateful to God for your _____ (for example, conversation, treatment of my family, thinking of me, comfort, telling me how you feel).

3. Refer to a list of verses that affirm truths about your identity in Christ (Appendix 2a). Which ones catch your attention? Why?

4. Use the prayer taken from Psalm 139 (Appendix 3). Insert the name of your spouse or another person whom you find difficult to love and add the appropriate pronouns. Spend time praying over this person with the completed psalm.

5. The Hebrew word 'ārûm, translated "cunning or crafty," (Genesis 3:1) is sandwiched between two instances of 'ārôm, meaning "naked." Notice the only difference is one vowel. What is it that changed between the first "nakedness" that was without shame and the second "nakedness" that Adam and Eve tried to hide? The entrance of the Serpent and sin. Satan takes the good of God's design, intended to reflect His faithfulness and provision, and turns it into something that destroys.

Identify a way evil can creep into your marriage and family life that then distances you from God and from each other (for example, vain imaginings adopted as truth or that have become a stockpiled arsenal, assumptions that question motivation and intent). Be specific as you identify elements of spiritual warfare threatening your marriage, family, reputations, and conferences.

Transformational

1. How can I be praying for you and the members of your team?

2. Exchange your thoughts on how being grateful changes your soul. Be specific.

3. Which are the most difficult truths to accept about your identity in Christ? Why do you think that is so? What part of your internal story might need a gentle corrective to align with God's truth of who you already are in Him?

4. Continue your conversation with God with reflections from your time of praying Psalm 139 over someone. What changes in your own soul are you beginning to sense God orchestrating?

5. In what ways will you each be vigilant in combatting the twisted untruths that threaten your marriage? (For example, knowing more of God's Word, prayer, listening to understand, conference.) Be specific.

CHAPTER 9

FROM PASTOR TO PEW
AND BACK AGAIN

Public preaching speaks to more, but with less advantage to each individual.

Richard Baxter, *Reformed Pastor*

It will be by private conference when we have an opportunity to set all home for the conscience and the heart.

Richard Baxter, *Reformed Pastor*

SOUL-TO-SOUL PURPOSE

"Physicians of the Soul" describes an important aspect of Puritan pastors' responsibilities. Their practice of conference was both common and expected. As this means of conference continued, it became an integral part of the life of the church. Nicholas Bownd comments from Malachi 2:7, "The people ought to confer with the Minister, and he with them, and they with one another."[1] There was an expectation that pastors would conference with those who had questions about their faith (or lack of it), who were experiencing spiritual doubts, or those whose challenging life situations compelled them to seek godly counsel. Conference provided the venue for assessing understanding of biblical truth as well as discussing the appropriate application of those truths.

The plain and powerful ministry of preaching was understood to be the primary means to prepare a heart for Christ, as skilled preachers summoned persons to conversion and holiness. Beyond the pulpit, however, was a network of private communication where individuals revealed and shared their spiritual health.[2] Both seekers and believers desired to have spiritual conversations with their pastors and others whose spiritual maturity and experience extended beyond their own. Seekers wanted to know more about the Christian faith, oftentimes having been convicted by a truth heard in a sermon message. Believers facing various challenges, trials, and doubts sought counsel from fellow believers who had grown familiar with their life stories. Both types of pilgrims were impacted by hearing sermons, reviewing sermon notes, and conversing with pastors and godly believers.

SOUL-TO-SOUL PERSPECTIVE

Deepening introspection, brought about by sermons and conversations with pastors and mature believers, is necessary to acknowledge the presence of grace in a seeker's life. Baxter was particularly attentive to the seeker. Of all people, the nonbeliever should not be ignored: "He that sees a man of a mortal disease, and another only pained with the toothache, will be moved more to compassionate the former, than the latter, and will surely make more haste to help him."[3]

When conversion is understood as a regenerative process, and not an event, conference plays an integral part of preconversion and conversion. Conference helps to address the questions, doubts, misunderstandings, and false assumptions people have. Baxter's sentiments are found in his commitment to conference with the nonbeliever, "You know we cannot speak so familiarly, and come so close to every one's case in a common sermon as we may do by conference . . . and therefore I entreated you to allow me now and then an hour's set and sober talk with you, when all other matters might for that time be laid by."[4]

Baxter found so great a number of those coming to faith through preaching, private conferences, and conversations about the state of their souls that he deemed conference, together with instructions on the principles of the Christian faith, a great necessity.

When meeting with believers, the spiritually mature have "a willing and ready mind in them, to satisfy them privately by conference, who should resort to them upon special need and occasion, to comfort them in their heaviness, and to stir them up to religious and godly communication in their meetings privately, and at their table."[5] Christian leaders, as counselors of souls, expect and welcome believers with life's conundrums and challenges. These opportunities help to assess the spiritual health of those in our churches, communities, and small groups.

SOUL-TO-SOUL PARTICIPANTS

Pastors encouraged congregants to conference with ministers and other experienced Christians and to glean from "learned men's writings" that shed light on and gave understanding to Scripture. The role of a pastor or wise friend who gently guides the soul is imperative. These conversations are more than brief exchanges of pleasantries. They are substantive and carried out with earnestness.

Thomas Tregosse, a Puritan pastor, was known to take any and all convenient opportunities to inquire of others' eternal estate. His exercise of conference with those in his household extended to others, as he was "endowed and invested with a singular gift of personal conference, which talent he carefully employed for the good of many souls." He would pose questions to those whom he led to Christ and desired the same from them.[6]

|||||||||||||||||||||||||||||||||||||||||

HISTORICAL SNAPSHOT

Thomas Tregosse (c. 1670–1671) was silenced in 1662 and prohibited from preaching in a public place. He was remembered for his gift of conference, pressing others to holiness through questions posed in conversations or by turning unedifying conference to a more holy discourse.

Pastors hold a prominent role in guiding people to conversion, but alongside this must be added the influence of an extended community. Not only is conversion a lengthy process, it is also a multifaceted experience. Believers are not to be concerned only with their own salvation and growth in grace and holiness; they have also an obligation to the unregenerate in offering them salvation in Christ.

Seekers too are encouraged to conference as a means to come to a saving knowledge of God. This is accomplished by asking questions of believers and ministers in order to gain understanding, resolve doubts, and call to memory truths which may have been forgotten.

SOUL-TO-SOUL PERKS

As pastors and ministry leaders add diligent visitation and conference with those in their congregations, they gain a deeper understanding of the spectrum of their members' life stages and circumstances. When those who serve their church community become more familiar with fellow Christians, these believers in turn are encouraged and inclined to reveal their doubts and worries to their leaders. The counsel and consolation received is of great comfort knowing others have experienced these same trials and yet are now strong in faith.

The time given to inquire after the spiritual states of members affords leaders opportunities to know their congregations better personally. Invaluable information gleaned from these encounters can impact a leader's service both directly and indirectly. Direct one-with-one encounters allow a leader the personal contact that exhibits his or her shepherding gifts. These encounters can also help facilitate the minister in sermon preparation and delivery. Public preaching becomes better understood and regarded. Baxter adds,

> By means of it [conference], we shall come to be better acquainted with each person's spiritual state, and so the better know how to watch over them . . . We shall know better how to preach to them . . . we shall know better how to lament for them, and to rejoice for them, and to pray for them.[7]

The resulting messages become less detached from everyday life and more in touch with the spiritual hunger and painful and perplexing experiences of the listeners. Being more in tune with the spiritual journey's roadblocks, detours, pitfalls, and victories can highlight truths from Scripture and enable the pastor to teach with grace, empathy, and direction. John R. W. Stott offers sound advice on this type of engagement:

> The best preachers are always diligent pastors, who know the people of their district and congregation, and understand the human scene in all its pain and pleasure, glory and tragedy. And the quickest way to gain such an understanding is to shut our mouth (a hard task for compulsive preachers) and open our eyes and ears. . . . We need, then, to ask people questions and get them talking. We ought to know more about the Bible than they do, but they are likely to know more about the real world than we do. So we should encourage them to tell us about their home and family life, their job, their expertise and their spare-time interests. We also need to penetrate beyond their doing to their thinking.[8]

Pastors better knowing their communities can produce more engaging and relevant preaching.

As pastors grow more sensitive to the needs of their congregations, they can facilitate and seek to replicate care and concern among other leaders in the church. Pastors who have experienced this kind of conference, both receiving and extending it, are more inclined to promote, encourage, and offer verbal, moral, and prayerful support, and to seek financial resources for training leaders.

Leaders understand that the effectiveness of biblical preaching and conferencing is dependent upon the strengthening and sanctifying grace of God's Spirit. They also see the need to grow in knowledge of the Scriptures and to care for others' souls. The pastoral care and guidance given in conference to another's soul is grounded in knowledge of the Holy Spirit's commitment to our growth in authenticity and His dissatisfaction with the complacency and fraud of counterfeit faith. The benefits to those involved at all levels of engagement in and outside the church will be deep and wide-ranging.

SOUL-TO-SOUL PAUCITY

Conference with wise and experienced pastors can limit misconceptions and misconstructions of the Christian faith that have unfortunate results. Those who lack knowledge of God and His Word, yet claim to speak for Him, communicate inaccurate and distorted beliefs. An undiscerning audience, even of

Christ followers, can inadvertently accept and adopt untruths or false teachings. Such ignorance, when translated into error-prone behavior and deeds, misrepresents the Trinity, God's Word, His kingdom, and His disciples.

A growing understanding of God through His Word and His people, or at least a curiosity about these matters, needs to be met with wise counsel and biblical guidance. This can be addressed in conversations that welcome questions, doubts, and inquiries. These questions may range from the simple to the complex, but when opportunities present themselves, they must be addressed. When one cultivates the willingness to be available, opportunities will present themselves.

A lack of personal instruction and conference can lead to missed opportunities for evangelism, salvation, edification, and needed encouragement. Even and perhaps especially amid the culture of social media, people are discovering unmet needs in the challenges of life and longing for help from a healthy community. Additionally, if identity formation for human beings is designed to be cultivated in the context of a biblically sound, soul-enhancing community, many will find themselves questioning aspects of themselves without the knowledge of where to seek that guidance, direction, and support.

||||||||||||||||||||||||||||||||||||||||||

HISTORICAL SNAPSHOT

Francis Rous (1579–1659) was a lay Puritan, religious writer, and politician. Rous's desire for reform of the English church, which influenced his contributions to Parliament, attested to his integration of theology and politics.

Francis Rous, an English politician and a prominent Puritan, pens, "And indeed when the soul is in the dark, and her own light shines not, she may do well to get a guide, and to take heed to borrowed light, until the day dawn, and the daystar arises in her own heart."[9] Though sermons serve as an initial entry point toward grace, at any given point, support from pastors and others who offer biblical counsel can minister needed grace.

SOUL-TO-SOUL PREPARATION

You will know if an environment is conducive to people's openness to talk when they begin to ask for your time. It is an indication they are willing to take a risk and let someone see a glimpse of their true self, masked behind their false self meant for public consumption. Counter the temptation to be busy enough to avoid engagement. Get to know the stories of those whom you serve; you will serve better.

Gathering people for the sole purpose of introducing themselves to each other is a nonthreatening way to begin to hear stories. Such a gathering may be a precursor to a small group Bible study, but it is not a small group Bible study at this stage. It promotes a genuine acceptance of people without necessitating the forming of a group and creates a primer for relationship development and early conversations where asking questions or sharing concerns can follow.

Cultivating an environment of acceptance while addressing questions can also be instituted in a Sunday service. Doing so will involve working smarter. Few Christian communities have unlimited budgets or volunteers, so start broadly. Ask your church attenders to text questions they might have during a Sunday service. Enlist the help of one or two wise leaders and discuss appropriate responses to relevant questions. Carve out a few minutes of the following service to respond. This can be a fun and informative practice, while creating an environment of openness to questions of various kinds. For those who find it difficult to approach leaders with questions, this approach can provide an easier way to having a burning question answered. It also sets the stage for seeking a more personal discussion at a later time. The anonymous questioner is valued and others are encouraged to participate without fear of being ignored, belittled, or embarrassed.

A network of shepherds, lay community pastors, and mature, godly saints among your congregants can be employed. It will be important as a pastor to meet with them and they with each other to assess and evaluate these efforts in connecting and caring for people. Your reach and that of your leadership team is extended through these volunteers.

SOUL-TO-SOUL PROMPTS

Whether you are a pastor, ministry leader, believer, or seeker, no one expects you to do life alone. The design for every human being includes community. And no one expects you to know and experience God without someone coming alongside you. As we do so, it is important to remember the difference between caring and curing. Ray Anderson observes,

> There is too often a "get well soon" message hidden in many of our attempts to help someone with whom we live when they have a problem or share some pain. This is especially true if we become anxious when someone we care about does not respond to our attempts to help. When caring becomes associated with curing, we do not know how to care for persons when their pain seems incurable. Sometimes caring means allowing a person space to be oneself within the bond of friendship, without expecting that person to "get well" as a condition of being accepted.[10]

To care without the expectation of curing affects the quality of conference by pastors and spiritual and ministry leaders in large and small groups and friendships.

SEEKER

Informational

1. "It's good to see you (again)." Sometimes you will be sought out as a pastor or leader, and other times you will be given an opportunity to exercise biblical hospitality, extending friendship to a stranger. Express gratitude for the courage given someone to ask questions.

2. What seems to be the matter most pressing on your mind?

3. Listen to both the other person and the Holy Spirit.

4. If you were to describe God, what would He be like?

5. How would you describe the heart of a person? The soul?

Transitional

1. Whatever questions you might have about who this Jesus is, I would enjoy chatting with you about Him.

2. If this is a matter of need for forgiveness, weave into the conversation the humility and power of Jesus's sacrifice on the cross and the implications of His resurrection.

3. Affirm as you gently and briefly inquire why and where, unpacking the layers of feelings about a situation or relationship. Continue to listen intently as the heart is revealing itself. You may then be able to present God's perspective or movement in kindness-lined truth. This will always be consistent with His written Word.

   ◉ It seems that God may be saying/moving _____.
   ◉ What are your thoughts?

4. How does this description align with God's revelation of Himself in His Word? Consider assigning homework. Recommend Scripture passages to be read that help the seeker discover what God reveals of Himself and who Jesus is.

5. Why would God be concerned with a person's heart and soul?

Transformational

1. Tell your own story of having been transferred from darkness into God's kingdom of light. The gospel (good news) is God's triumph over sin and all its destructive effects through Christ's death and resurrection. The mystery of our participation in God's redemptive plan through faith in Him gives evidence that our transformation rests on the gospel.

2. End with prayer and words of gratitude for this person and their time.

3. Forgiveness is not the approval of an act, but it is the releasing of the bitterness that can paralyze the forgiver. May I pray for you and those involved?

4. Listen for the words a person uses that acknowledge God's involvement or truth. Note these as you pray.

5. Review the seeker's discoveries and answer questions, while instilling the curiosity to discover more about God from His Word.

6. Affirm the seeker's right thoughts about the heart and soul with truths of God's intimate knowledge of their heart and soul.

BELIEVER

Informational

1. "How is your walk with God?" Listen to both the other person and the Holy Spirit.

2. Where is your health barometer registering?

3. Though I may not be able to give you a clear answer for the direction you should go, know that from God's perspective, the process is as important if not more important than the outcome. What might it look like to explore that process together?

4. How is fear manifested in your life? Consider assigning homework. The process of recording thoughts and feelings can help reduce the vicious cycles of worry and fear, and can begin to add order and truth to your thinking. List current worries and fears in one column and instances where God proved present and faithful in the second. What thoughts are associated with your fears? Be as specific as you can.

5. What are the symptoms of anger in your life? If the soul is both body and spirit, the whole person, what are the effects of this anger on your soul?

Transitional

1. Affirm as you gently and briefly inquire why and where, unpacking the layers of feelings that reveal the knowledge held regarding a situation or relationship. Continue to listen intently as the heart is revealing itself. You may then be able to present

God's perspective or movement in kindness-lined truth. This will always be consistent with His written Word.

- ◉ It seems that God may be saying/moving _____.
- ◉ What are your thoughts?

2. These circumstances must be weighing heavily on your heart. How are you coping? What is the most difficult part?

3. Difficult decisions that have multiple options can be perplexing, especially when most options appear good. What has your discernment process looked like?

4. God designed our lives to be lived out in peace, trusting Him in all circumstances. Homework: What does God reveal about Himself in His Word that is meant to help you combat fear and to trust Him more? How big is your God? If He is small, then you have every reason to doubt and fear, but if He is as He reveals Himself in His Word, then you can begin to rest in that truth. He is big enough for your fears.

5. Consider assigning homework. Allow God to bring to mind the triggers that fuel your anger. Record these.

Transformational

1. Pray. Listen for the words a person uses that acknowledge God's involvement or truth. Note these and pray.

2. How have you been here before?

- ◉ The circumstances may be different, but the pattern of what God is doing may be the same. How so?
- ◉ How did God show Himself faithful to you at that time?

3. How might He want to prove Himself worthy of your trust once again?

4. In the Red Sea *versus* Jordan River moments in your life, God

sometimes clearly marks the path to follow. At other times, He requires you to take a step into the water before the path becomes clear. Describe the one God has placed before you and how His Spirit is wanting to navigate you.

- What has God placed right in front of you that He is wanting you to address but can so easily be sideswiped by a pressing matter (or oppressing matter) that steals your attention away from His sovereign peace-giving guidance?
- How might you be open to an option (God's) not even considered yet?

5. From what you know of Jesus, what is He saying? What can you thank God for in acknowledging His presence and provision? Be specific.

6. Review homework with observations and affirmation of biblical truths, helping to unpack the layers of past hurts or lies that have perpetuated the emotional reaction of anger.

CHAPTER 10

NOT YOUR TYPICAL
PASTORS CONFERENCE

*I was well refreshed, recovered my desire to study
and willingness to renew my Christian course, and
returning home, all the way home, I most joyfully
was occupied in thinking of God's merciful dealing
with me [in] many ways.*

Richard Rogers, *Two
Elizabethan Puritan Diaries*

SOUL-TO-SOUL PURPOSE

Centuries ago, the practice of conference served to help pastors as they met with other pastors. Conference for groups of Puritan pastors included times for an exchange of ideas, which proved necessary amid the critical need for supplemental education of godly clergy. After these public homiletical exercises, which served to sharpen their own preaching skills, pastors withdrew to another place to engage in fraternal review of the sermons and of their personal lives and morals. Not only did these gatherings cultivate a strong sense of belonging to their fellow colleagues, but the advice, support, mutual encouragement, fellowship, and sociability exchanged provided sustenance for these like-hearted ministers, especially in seasons of stress and doubt.[1]

Both a pastor's personal study of God's Word and sermon preparation are influenced by conference. Because the primary responsibility of a Puritan pastor was to teach God's Word, conference was a necessity for that charge. Richard Baxter charged his readers to "Study, and pray, and confer, and practice; for in these four ways your abilities must be increased."[2] His conviction was evident in his establishing regular meetings of like-minded clergy, where opportunities for conference, fellowship, and mutual encouragement through shared meals were offered.

|||||||||||||||||||||||||||||||||||||

HISTORICAL SNAPSHOT

Thomas Hooker (1586–1647) was an English-born minister in America. His messages against some church rituals brought him to the attention of Archbishop William Laud, who removed Hooker from his teaching post. Hooker impacted both England and New England.

Of particular interest is the outgrowth of mentoring relationships. Thomas Hooker, a prominent Pilgrim colonial leader, who founded the colony of Connecticut, was known for investing in the lives of the next generation of pastors, offering critical guidance and direction. Cotton Mather, an American minister, described an aspect of Hooker's ministry and influence:

> The godly ministers round about the country, would have recourse unto him to be directed and resolved in their *difficult cases*; and it was by his means that those godly ministers held their monthly meetings, for fasting and prayer, and profitable conferences. It was the effect of his consultations also, that such godly ministers came to be here and there settled in several parts of the country; and many others came to be better established in some great points of Christianity by being in his neighborhood and acquaintance.[3]

This pastor extended himself to a community of pastors, but would also meet with individuals. On an equally honoring note about Hooker, John Fuller (b. 1640 or 41) penned,

> We were of an intimate society and vicinity for many years, we took sweet counsel together, and walked unto the house of God in company. He was my guide, and my acquaintance, as David hath it. We oft breathed and poured out our souls together in prayer, fasting and

conferences. When walking after the Lord in a wilderness, we had less allowed liberty, but more inward enlarging of Spirit.[4]

Fuller writes of the "great mercy and unspeakable blessing" enjoyed by many in "the labors of that powerful, soul-saving, heart-searching minister."[5] Heart-searching. There is no doubt Hooker asked well-framed questions that connected biblical truths with soul care.

The investment of an older minister's time and attention into the lives of younger ministers portrays a cross-generational commitment. Richard Baxter was a recipient of such an investment. He was influenced by several godly pastors "whose fervent prayers, and savory *Conferences* and holy lives did profit me much."[6]

Ministers were also found to have enjoyed conference in closer relationships as described by Richard Rogers. A diary entry described the conference he had with neighboring minister and friend Ezekiel Culverwell, "For it is not out of season at any time, to be occupied either in conference about knowledge attaining or growing in godliness. . . . And this shall be one of the greatest stays unto my heavy heart, if it may please the Lord to continue this benefit unto us."[7] Rogers received transformational spiritual guidance in his relationship with Culverwell, a man known to be powerful in conference. Rogers knew from his own meditation and the advice of his friend how the ideals of godliness could be manifested.

SOUL-TO-SOUL PERSPECTIVE

Pastors have full and busy schedules. Between their own study of the Scriptures and sermon preparation, they must be available to offer spiritual counsel, meet for premarital counseling sessions, perform weddings and funerals, attend community events, arrange for hospital or home visitations, teach baptism classes, provide leadership to the pastoral and ministry staff, lead staff meetings and address organizational concerns, review Sunday or weekend services (past, present, and future), *and* care for their own families. These schedules are indeed full, but upon closer review, they are plagued with "doing" activities with little or no priority for opportunities to develop "being." This unhealthy prioritization manifests itself in the soul and affects surrounding relationships. When one's identity focuses on the "doing" aspects of ministry, accolades and accomplishments have a greater addictive draw than the gain found in deepening personal Christlikeness. Pride is more likely to masquerade in ministry achievements and successes. And as confidently as one may feel about the veiled pride, it exposes itself in some form or another over time.

Pastors often feel the pressure to be "on guard" around people and thus keep a safe distance from people. Internalizing negative feedback on sermon messages, counseling approaches, and financial decisions amid the demands of leadership make fostering deep relationships difficult. Resulting friendships are few and shallow. Research finds that pastors' satisfaction with their friendships is on par with or only slightly better than US adults overall. They are also more likely than the general public to feel lonely and isolated from others. Younger pastors, those in their thirties and forties, seem to have a harder time making friends and feeling connected. These and other factors can rank some as high-risk pastors, those who may be prone to experience burnout, relational difficulty, and spiritual setbacks. Pastors need friends.[8] They, as much as those in the pews, need shepherding and nurturing along their faith journeys. Godliness takes honest assessment and forthright guidance—and lots of each. To grow in their love for God and others, for the church and for the Church, will require a confidant who is not only a good sounding board but who also values and models confidentiality, godly wisdom, humility, and grace.

Whether it is with an older, more mature mentor or in peer mentoring, pastors benefit from having trusted spiritual friends. A measure of the trust found in these relationships can be noted in the lack of pressure to be theologically correct as one processes life's challenges and doubts. Mutual accountability, and more importantly, mutual attentiveness to one another's hearts, is critical. This may sometimes involve difficult yet necessary conversations where "Tell me what I need to hear, not just what I want to hear" is humbly spoken with courage. Wisdom is found in Proverbs 15:31, "One who listens to life-giving rebukes will be at home among the wise." This depth of engagement and commitment to conference between two colleagues is mutually beneficial and stands as grounds for its continued use.

SOUL-TO-SOUL PARTICIPANTS

Conference serves to foster discussions of personal and corporate interest and importance. This practice has two expressions: pastors meeting with members of their congregations and ministers gathering with one another. The first was addressed in the previous chapter.

Seeking a trusted spiritual friend, peer mentor, or older mentor starts with prayer and a sincere desire that reflects a humble need for a strength-giving relationship. Consider these factors as you are guided in your search. Spiritual friends, typically other pastors or ministry leaders, may be found both within and outside of the pastor's own church boundaries. Spiritually sensitive elder board members or fellow staff pastors can be readily accessible and observant. Other possibilities can include but are not limited to those serving in denominational organizations, para-church organizations, campus ministries, or Christian service organizations. Remember to consider Christian business leaders, seminary professors, groups of ministry leaders from different churches, and fellow seminary friends and graduates. Even if these friendship opportunities occur naturally, seeking such relationships will require your purposeful resolve and alertness to God's leading.

The initial "ask" is probably the most daunting. Here's a start:

- Introduce or re-introduce yourself, if needed.
- Briefly explain why you are approaching this particular person.
- Briefly state what you hope to learn.
- Comment on the type of honesty you would like to achieve.
- Offer appreciation for the consideration.

This is a significant way to honor someone who is older and who can offer wisdom drawn from more of life's experiences and seasons.

A spiritual friend or mentor is more than a sounding board, a kick in the pants, or a shoulder to cry on. This person reflects Christ in their own context, be it church, family, marketplace, sports team, and the like. The main goal is not to have a mentee or friend become dependent on you, but for each person involved to grow more dependent on the love of God, the grace of Christ, and the power of His Spirit. Take these suggestions under consideration as you think through investing in another's life as a spiritual friend or mentor:

- Pray. This is the first step in being deliberate toward establishing this relationship.
- You set the parameters and the tone. This includes how long, often the purpose, and time and place you will meet, while committing to pray with and for each other and the relationship at and between meetings.
- The "ask" is not for perfection but presence; it is not about having all the answers but is for attentiveness.
- Keep it simple. Be yourself. Be real. Really. How you navigate through the mundane and the madness of life is life-giving. Some mentees need to see what healthy (not perfect) family relationships and environments are like. Your willingness to open your life and calendar establishes, builds, and maintains transparency, trust, and empathy.
- Interceding for and impacting another brings about growth in God's kingdom, manifesting His reign in our lives. As much of our church culture is focused on leadership, more attention needs to be directed to godly follower-ship.
- Your experiences may be just what God designed to complement another's life and another's experiences may be just what God designed to complement your life, as you both grow in being like Christ to one another. Mentoring is not a spotlight ministry and thus fosters Christlike humility.
- Your mentee will benefit as much from the well-framed questions for self-reflection you ask as the wisdom and perspective you impart. You might, as well. Some conversations need not be ministry related at all.
- Challenge, counter, and combat the distancing, fragmentation, speed, isolationism, and individualism our culture promotes but has been found unsatisfying. Expect challenges. Make a difference. You will.

C. S. Lewis's perspective is simple and true: "Think of me as a fellow-patient in the same hospital who, having been admitted a little earlier, could give some advice."[9]

SOUL-TO-SOUL PERKS

Reflecting on meeting with another pastor in an informal setting, Richard Rogers penned, "After conference . . . In my return home my mind by the way was taken up in very heavenly sort, rejoicing not a little that the Lord had so enlarged my heart as that my old and accustomed dreams and fantasies of things below were vanished and drowned."[10] Conference between pastors and ministry leaders restores hope and encourages in times of challenge and difficulty. The refreshment and renewed clarity of direction experienced through conference produced gratefulness to God for His mercy and provision, a familiar result from the exercise of this means of grace. Gary A. has a conference relationship with his pastor and testifies to this in his reflection:

> It would take a book to tell the ways my colleague has encouraged me and my house. When we began ministry many years ago it became very evident that he was working from a changed heart, a heart that had been discipled by many before him. His testimony and actions stirred me for more. Although we moved to different parts of the country I still have the ability to call on him for encouragement and direction in the Word. In the past years I have taken much of what I have learned and shared with others, who in turn have done the same. The impact of true conference has changed the way I approach the gospel and others.

This also gives opportunity for (what I call) theological jam sessions and reflecting on how theological truths apply to living an impacting life. Safe places where pastoral hearts can be attended are created and sustained. Though mutually beneficial for those who engage in pastoral conference, there are other positive side effects.

The benefits of conference need not be limited to godly conversations between pastors and ministry leaders. Some needed life-giving refreshment can be received when engaging in conference with those other than fellow pastors or ministry partners. Rogers recorded a time when he wrestled with a sense of unwillingness to attend to his work, so he sought out his neighbor:

> I found good stirring up of my mind by our conference, which seldom is, at our particular meetings, without some sensible fruit and blessing, that though we were at that time more than commonly heavy for some unsettledness, yet, I thank God, I was well refreshed, recovered my desire to study and willingness to renew my Christian course.[11]

When those in a congregation discover that their leaders engage in regular conferencing with mentors or spiritual friends, it builds trust in the leadership, validates community, and encourages congregants to consider having spiritual friends or having and being mentors themselves. There is also a sense of assurance in knowing that their pastor seeks wisdom and is receiving soul care. This reduces the potential for moral failure or being a "lone ranger," "loose-cannon-on-deck," or "solo" leader. Pastors know how much easier it is to slip into life-denying autonomy than to step into the gift of God-given, grace-receiving, calling-restoring community. When they intentionally move toward this kind of community, however, congregants have been known to notice and appreciate their pastor becoming more approachable and open to their concerns, while also becoming more vulnerable.

A little closer to home, your family may benefit when conference is employed in mentoring and spiritual friendships. As a wife of a pastor, Donna B. observes,

> Jeff's mutually encouraging relationships with men that God has placed in his life have proved to be a consistent source of encouragement, sounding board, and resource in his life. If he has ever had a need or there has been an issue that he was struggling with, those men have always been there to shoulder the load. These relationships have kept him fresh in his walk with the Lord and on the cutting edge of his faith.

This concept of conference impacts me (and our kids) by knowing that those relationships will always be there for him and, as a result, gives me security, confidence, and assurance that he will remain faithful and stay the course for the long haul. This has also made him a better husband, father, and man which has had a huge impact on our family.

God-given friendships allow truthful voices to be heard outside the marriage or family context that offer refreshment, perspective, and wise counsel. These voices also become a second line of defense in the battle against temptation and sin, and in recognizing many and any crippling addictions, legal or illegal, be it the magnetism of illicit drugs or the more culturally acceptable yet subtle obsessions with pride, popularity, financial gain, comparison, or fear. Some pastors find their spouses commenting on their improved demeanor after such godly conversations.

Conference can be contagious and curative.

SOUL-TO-SOUL PAUCITY

Puritan pastors noted a number of observable symptoms that can reveal unattended souls in and among them. Richard Rogers writes, "We spoke of . . . how hardly we enter into watchful[ness] over ourselves against any inward or outward evil, and how soon we wax weary of that course."[12] Rogers' spiritual friend and fellow pastor, Ward, adds these to the list: "troubled by roving thoughts, and spiritual dullness, the failure to be 'fruitful' in talking religion to his companions, and by the neglect of his duties as student and teacher, pride, anger, adulterous thoughts, and lack of charity."[13] How easy it is to slip into spiritual weariness.

Pastor and author Bob Burns offers some contemporary observations:

- A factual knowledge of the Bible and theology does not equal spiritual maturity. Many people preparing for the ministry abandon spiritual disciplines while in training. They may put aside Bible study from the rhythm of their daily lifestyle.
- Pastors often fail to seriously reflect on their spiritual lives.

- Pastor: What happens when I skirt my spiritual growth? I replace it with the "spiritual" tasks of pastoral life.
- We grow busier and busier to please more and more people. We spend more time in meetings than we do in prayer.[14]

Peter Scazzero, pastor, author, and co-founder of Emotionally Healthy Spirituality, says, "Work 'for' God that is not nourished by a deep interior life 'with' God will eventually be contaminated [polluted] by other things such as ego, power, needing approval of and from others, and buying into the wrong ideas of success and the mistaken belief that we can't fail."[15] The potential to live autonomous and discombobulated lives is real and still too common. There is a vital need for godly conversations that impact the souls of pastors.

SOUL-TO-SOUL PREPARATION

It was understood that Puritan pastors were both preacher and teacher, but it was expected they would be spiritual guides of human souls as well. Direction was needed to help navigate the challenges and complexities of life. John Brown recognizes the posture required to give this level of guidance. He pens,

> Some men who are not ministers have this gift, and there are ministers who have it not. There is a divine art in dealing with men not to be learnt all at once, not to be acquired in lecture halls or from books, but on your knees in communion with God, and in the daily experiences of life in living sympathy with men. It comes only in its fullness with the process of years, and with deepening heart experiences of our own. It requires a large and varied knowledge of men, their motives, their sorrows, their temptations.[16]

An intimate relationship, comfortable and familiar with being present before God and present before others, is foundational in offering counsel and guidance. Grow your relationship with God and others in learning to be still and quiet. Heed God's invitations to be with Him in regular, dedicated time in silence and solitude. Share your reflections with a trusted friend. It will not be a waste of time.

One must also beware of a couple myths that keep pastors from seeking the influence of the godly wise:

- *Pastors are exempt from the need for soul care.* The calling and training of a pastor does not preclude them from the need for a healthy community and for a carefully select few to speak into their lives, to be attentive to their hearts and souls.
- *Factual knowledge of the Bible and theology equals spiritual maturity.* Spiritual maturity is the outgrowth of biblical truth plus life experience. One does not equal the other. Each supports the other in life-affirming truth. They are mutually instructive and enlightening.

Desiring and exercising conference can diffuse these myths and supply pastors with needed care in genuine relationships. Souls are enriched and lives are well sustained when ministry servants are supported in trusted friendships.

SOUL-TO-SOUL PROMPTS

There are times when these prompts may require more thought and reflection. Give pastors additional time to ponder them between your meetings.

Informational

1. What has been a highlight of your week? A lowlight? Who was associated with each?

2. What has been a nagging fear you have for yourself? For your family? For your ministry?

3. Identify a personal strength. Identify a personal weakness.

4. On a scale of 1–10, rate your prayer life. Explain your score.

5. This one is a tough one. Identify a moment when you chose to be distracted by the radio, T.V., a movie, or the internet.

6. What justice issue, small or grand, gets under your skin?

7. How often do you find yourself thinking about church attendance numbers or people leaving your church?

Transitional

1. What emotions were associated with that highlight? Lowlight?

2. What fuels each fear?

3. How has God used a strength? How has He brought about dependence on Him because of a weakness?

4. On what do your prayers tend to focus—adoring God? Confessing to Him? Thanking Him? Asking Him for things?

5. What was going on in your mind when that happened? What were you thinking about in the split seconds before you turned to that device?

6. What "holy discontent," to cite a well-known book title, might He be stirring in your heart?

7. How would your life and ministry be morphed if growth was measured in being Christ-centered and others-focused versus church attendance numbers, personal achievements and accolades, or how your church stacks up against another?

Transformational

1. What truths of God being the giver of good gifts do you receive?

2. What truths of God being a present help (Psalm 46:1), preserving the bruised reed and smoldering wick (Isaiah 42:3) can you receive? Or is this difficult to accept? Why?

3. "Fear not" is one of the most prominent commands found in the

Bible. If fear is looking into the future without God in it, what fears have captured more of your thoughts than you would like?

4. Matthew and Luke show that the Evil One tempts Jesus when and where He is weak, but he also tempts Jesus where He is strong. What are some subtle and not-so-subtle temptations directed toward your strengths? Your weaknesses? How might your identity be wrapped up in your strengths?

5. On your own, spend thirty minutes in prayer and refrain from asking God for anything. Record your reflections. What did you discover about your prayers? Your relationship with God in prayer?

6. What is it that God wants you to give to Him in order for you to have real peace and wisdom, building trust in Him and allowing Him to prove his faithfulness to you?

7. What prayers is God wanting to answer as you seek Him for your involvement in this matter?

8. Why do these matters take so much of your time, attention, and energy? Take it to prayer. Put it in written words and share this with a trusted friend.

Remember, each of these prompts has its Informational, Transitional, and Transformational sequence. Give time to listen, process, unpack, and respond. The best responses are considerate, having thoughtful silences, pauses, facial expressions, nonverbal postures, spoken words, and sometimes tears. You are connecting biblical truth with soul care—connecting God with one uniquely made in His image. He is present in your meeting together as you manifest His care.

CHAPTER 11

DISTANCE CONFERENCING: FROM SIGNED LETTERS TO STREAMING SUNDAY SERVICES[1]

But yet considering some passages in your last and former letters concerning your spiritual condition, and knowing by experience in my self the reality of such complaints, I would not be so graceless as to neglect you wholly therein: And though I can say or do very little, yet a word or two might be of some use; nor do I know what guilt might lie upon me, if I should be silent or slight in this case! And therefore [Dear—] if my barren heart would suffer me, I would present you with a few words, as if you and I were alone in a corner in the presence of God.[2]

Jonathan Mitchel

SOUL-TO-SOUL PURPOSE

Puritans conferenced in various contexts, as we have seen: small groups, at home between parents and children and between spouses, pastors and spiritual leaders with seekers or believers, and pastors with pastors. Not all the instances of conference exercised by the English Puritans, however, involved face-to-face encounters. When distance separated friends and family, letter writing met the needs for communicating affections, updates, spiritual concerns, counsel, and exhortations.

Letter writing was a common form of communicating spiritual counsel, especially with the absence of nearby pastors or guides. As John Calvin extended his pastoral care through letters, the Puritans would follow in that practice. They would have perceived such spiritual guidance as needed and necessary.

Richard Sibbes, a Puritan pastor known as one of the greatest of spiritual physicians, penned,

> *I understand by your letter, that you have many and great trials; some external and bodily, some internal and spiritual: as the deprival of inward comfort, the buffetings (and that in more than ordinary manner) of your soul, with Satan's temptations: and (which makes all those inward and outward, the more heavy and insupportable) that you have wanted Christian society with the Saints of God, to whom you might make known your griefs, and by whom you might receive comfort from the Lord and encouragement in your Christian course.* [3]

Sibbes continues in his letter to offer counsel, admonishment, and challenge, before concluding his letter with this very personal intercessory closing,

> *So shall the peace of God ever establish you, and the God of peace ever preserve you; which is the prayer of*
>
> > *Your remembrancer at the*
> > *Throne of Grace*
> >
> > R. *Sibs*"[4]

From prison, Puritan pastor Joseph Alleine encourages the "endeared Christians" in Taunton,

> *I have no great felicity under God, than to serve the good of souls. Brethren beloved, How fares it with your souls? are they in health?*

do they prosper? I wish your temporal prosperity. It is a joy to hear when your trade doth flourish: But these are but very little things if we look into eternity. Brethren, my ambition for you is, that you should be cedars among the shrubs, that from you should sound out the Word of the Lord, and that in every place your Faith to God-ward should be spread abroad.[5]

HISTORICAL SNAPSHOT

Joseph Alleine (1634–1668) was an English dissenting minister and spiritual writer. He was ejected from his parish for failing to accept the Act of Uniformity and was imprisoned for much of a year for preaching illegally.

He closes the letter by penning this humble farewell,

The messengers have forced me abruptly to end here: I can add no more, but my prayers to my counsels, and so commending you to God, and the Word of his Grace, I rest.

The servant well-willer of your Souls,

Jos. Alleine[6]

Neither the lack of physical presence nor the distance that separated many Puritans from each other diminished the longing for the depth of wisdom and encouragement that came from conference.

Brilliana Harley was a staunch Puritan known for the more than three hundred preserved letters to her husband and eldest son, Edward (Ned). Her letters were rich with religious overtones. One written in 1639 to Edward, as he attended Magdalen Hall, Oxford, urged her son to heed her counsel to pursue spiritual practices as a means toward godliness, particularly conference:

HISTORICAL SNAPSHOT

Brilliana Harley (d. 1643) was a staunch Puritan and a parliamentarian. The collection of approximately 375 letters sent to her husband and eldest son, Edward, offers clear evidence of domestic and maternal concerns in her married life, while also engaged in religious and political debates.

My dear Ned, omit not private duties, and stir up your self to exercise yourself in holy conference, beg of God to give you a delight in speaking and thinking of those things which are your eternal treasure. I many times think godly conference is as much neglected by God's children, as any duty. I am confident you will in no way neglect the opportunity of profiting in the ways of learning, and I pray God prosper your endeavors.[7]

Harley is conscious of the depth of knowledge obtained through conference and is attentive to Edward's need of it. Her concerns highlight the importance and essential nature of conference. No one should be without it, least of all her beloved son, to whom she sends these endearing words: "I pray God bless you and keep your heart close to Him, so that you may experimentally know the ways of God to be the best and pleasant way."[8]

This depth of religious tone and spiritual advice, as found in these and other collections of letters, encouraged believers. Practical application was almost an assumption in these letters, as was a desire to know God's Word and to hold to sound theology.

SOUL-TO-SOUL PERSPECTIVE

In a world of emails, text messages, video conferences, highlights, deletes, and sends, one can communicate with others more today than history has ever known. Yet the depth of quality does not compare to the vast quantity of communication flooding the cloud. When addressing matters of spiritual well-being and growth in godliness, nothing can substitute the personal like-heartedness of another human being. Even our intelligent personal assistant and knowledge navigator, Siri, knows that. Though one can ask her questions, seeking recommendations and suggestions, she will defer to a better source when it comes to spiritual matters. Arielle L., a former student of mine, meant to send this text message to her dad:

ARIELLE: *(doing voice-to-text in the car, narrating message but forgetting to first say that it's a text to Dad):* "*I think God's trying to tell me something, between my car breaking down and random*

health stuff coming up, like maybe I need to slow down, even at
the craziest point in the semester."
SIRI: *"I would suggest addressing your spiritual questions to*
someone who is more qualified, ideally a human."

Even Siri knows there are some things she is not capable of supplying. Humans are uniquely qualified, equipped, and gifted for this purpose, to be of spiritual help and guidance to another. As our world becomes smaller and more easily connected, it would seem our spiritual networking could mirror this connectivity. The ability to connect and stay connected has never been so available to so many people across so many cultures and lands, and the ability to do so with split-second speed. The use of various means of communication—emails, texts, tweets, video conferences, or posts—can bridge the distance between people in spiritually redeeming ways. As letters served to grow biblical knowledge and provide soul care among those in the Puritan era, so too there are ways of remaining connected for spiritual growth in contemporary times when distance separates.

SOUL-TO-SOUL PARTICIPANTS

A sampling of the Puritan pastors who took to pen and paper to convey biblical truths and soul care to those at a distance are noted above. Richard Sibbes, a moderate Puritan, was one of the most influential Puritan divines of the seventeenth century and a celebrated preacher and pastor. Joseph Alleine, was a Puritan minister and spiritual writer and, though unjustly jailed, refused to pay the fine and instead spent the time writing letters to the people of Taunton. Jonathan Mitchel, a powerful preacher and the son of Puritans, was born in England and migrated to Massachusetts at the age of eleven.

Lady Brilliana Harley was a Puritan and parliamentarian who engaged in several religious and political debates of the 1630s and 1640s. The collection of more than three hundred surviving letters written to her husband and her eldest son, Edward (Ned), reveal her zeal for and love for her faith and family. In the autumn of 1643 she bravely defended

Brampton Bryan Castle during a six-week siege, though it would fall the following spring. Harley wrote her last letter on October 9, just before her death on October 29, 1643.

Whether in the Puritan era or our current reality, there are those who display a commitment to bridge the distance divide, ensuring that biblical truths and spiritual care are communicated. They understood the wax and wane of spiritual growth and exercised the means of conference to help strengthen the faith of others. Despite the distance, and at times amid persecution, they trusted that their correspondences would be readily received and impactful. The humility of being a lifelong learner and the tenacity to commit to using whatever means to support and encourage others are displayed in the communications of those who exercised conference at a distance.

Technology can close the gap and foster conference in ministry, marketplace, family, and personal contexts. Interviews were conducted with those who intentionally foster spiritual conversations using various forms of technology. These included individual, ministry group, business group, and church contexts. The following observations were made.[9]

My friend Charles embraces the idea of *sobremesa*, the time spent around the table after lunch or dinner, talking with those with whom you have just shared a meal. This is a time to digest and savor both food and friendship. Between the times of *sobremesa*, he uses phone calls and text messages to stay connected with his friend who lives miles away. These conversations have a spiritual nature about them as the two dialogue on various philosophies and theologies impacting Christians and the church.

Yunski is the recruitment director and president of the alumni network of Global Leadership Development Institute (GLDI), a forty-day experience in personal transformation and "visioneering." Young adults are challenged individually and corporately toward grasping scriptural truths and cultivating a biblical worldview. Alumni from around the world have formed groups of five or more. These groups meet to further members' growth in Christlikeness, servant leadership, developing a global perspective, personal matters, and calling. There are both weekly and monthly Bible-related meetings. Some groups are gender-specific, some are not. Some have names for their groups, some do not. The groups last from forty days to twelve months. Leadership of the group is shared, and both men and women contribute and experience deeper levels of engagement and transparency. More of these groups are moving toward intentional spiritual engagement and the integration of faith in their individual walks with God. Though offline meetings are sporadic, as members grow closer through the video conferences, the desire to meet more often in person also grows.

Paul is an involved chair and Vice President with Convene, an organization designed to connect, equip, and inspire Christian CEOs and business owners in growing exceptional businesses, becoming higher-impact leaders, and serving God with significance. It achieves its mission by connecting and empowering CEOs with high-capacity peers in a nonjudgmental and confidential environment where they can help one another gain insight, experience business growth, have impact, and leave a strong legacy. Groups of eight to sixteen members meet in person monthly, where the chair leads and facilitates the group in four fields: faith, family, friends, and financials. Paul recognizes the need to establish a foundation of trust and credibility, and takes seriously an approach taught by John Maxwell, the author, speaker, and leadership expert: to exhibit competence, connection, and character. In addition to the monthly meetings, Paul's coaching is done face-to-face. Soon, "Convene Virtual Forum" will allow for CEOs to meet through video conferencing from anywhere in the world.

Meet the Leith Family. Greg and Shelley have five grown children, three of whom are married. Desiring to stay connected and after learning about the practice of conferencing, the Leith family embarked on conference at a distance. They meet approximately once per month to conference on Google Hangouts. Their now two-hour conference times on a Sunday evening are focused on personal sharing and prayer. These "Puritan phone calls" are endearingly referred to as the Leith Family Puritan Throwback Call.

Having considered the technology, human resources, and budget available, a growing number of churches extend their reach by live-streaming their services and having them available on demand. Churches can, however, establish a more personal outreach by establishing a pastoral presence during a live feed. This "online community pastor" can be regularly present in the chatroom to interact with viewers, being available to answer questions, direct inquiries, and pray. This involvement gives viewers a sense of care, recognition, and value—a taste of what goes on in the church—even when miles apart. The direct exchange between a viewer and a community pastor allows for both the viewer and the many "silent viewers" to gain a sense of the attention and regard extended by the church toward the online community. This can direct and encourage the viewer to eventually participate with the church body in a face-to-face context, or it may draw people in their own contexts and proximities together to form deeper relationships that develop into their own communities.

Over the past decade, a growing number of churches have been providing church services in digital formats. Some extend their reach globally and provide hosts whenever a service is broadcasted. These volunteers are available to interact with viewers. Outlines that better help the viewer track with the message and Bible verses addressed in that message are easily provided. Prompts for viewers and small group leaders offer biblical truths and promote the next steps for personal or group learning. Viewers are encouraged and equipped to start talking, thinking, sharing, praying, and doing. The church can intentionally extend its reach in a way that fosters conversations toward transformative spiritual growth.

Notice that all of the above scenarios involve some kind of offline meeting or a directive toward this. These align with the human need for the transforming intent and impact inherent in shared, embodied fellowship and friendships.

It is largely from these contexts that observations and experiences of soul-to-soul perquisites (such as being able to engage with those who may have distanced or disengaged themselves from the church or to remind them of the value of coming to physical church community), paucity, and preparation of conference at a distance are drawn.

SOUL-TO-SOUL PERKS

The rhythm of connecting is a gift, even when done virtually. Seizing opportunities and the convenience to take fuller advantage of connecting in the in-betweens does not allow spiritual conversations to be ignored or lost. Sustained growth in relationship with one another and with God finds value in the seemingly ordinariness of days. Beyond the face-to-face times, the additional time given to collect thoughts and perspectives adds to a phone, text, or video conference conversation. Well-framed and thoughtful questions can be asked as one reads or listens to what is said or not said. As trust and community are built, friendships, family identities, and workplace and ministry relationships are created, supported, and reinforced. The digital meetings between regular or sporadic personal face-to-face times help strengthen caring relationships.

Through distance conferencing, families can create more intentional time to know each other and to learn more of how members respond to one another, even those who may be geographically close by. This knowledge is especially grown through the processes of the mundane, where most of life happens, hearing spoken words and observing postures and gestures as we respond to one another. Thoughts of others move to the forefront of our minds; prayers for those navigating through the process become more frequent and specific and allow all to be more aware of each other's stories when we are able to be in one another's presence. Biblical counsel is not necessarily offered, but thoughtful questions can be asked to assist another's own thinking process, to get to a different place. These questions offer more to think about and further the process that, again, can be supported in prayer. Taking matters to prayer both in and outside of the conference times lessens the pressure to try to solve an issue.

Conversations then are not limited to those at periodic family gatherings where catching up is the primary focus and when time is more limited, and can thus be overwhelming. In a mutually affecting way, distance conferencing can be an encouragement to spur families to meet in person more often or to connect more intentionally when they do meet.

The flexibility in time and location that distance conferencing can offer is a reality. The limitations of global time zones and traditional meeting rooms are reduced. In addition, the ability to do this in the comfort of one's own home and in the comfort of one's own pajamas is an added perk. Technically, one need only be "presentable" from the waist up. This kidding (kind of) aside, there is a reward when investing in another's self-discovery "aha!" moments and life improvements. The growth of integrity and character is more energy-producing and less tiring than the alternative. Walking the talk is often associated with a conscious extension of graciousness toward one another, as each learns and applies God's Word to life experiences and their developing stories.

Churches who extend their online reach by having a pastor or volunteer present to "host" the service as it is being streamed offer care to their viewers in direct and indirect ways. Some report viewers asking about and then attending the physical campus of the church or asking for prayer, and others respond to a sermon message by asking to receive Christ as Lord and Savior. Some viewers discover through the chat that they are from the same area and offer to meet in person to watch the services together. The potential for numerical growth at a distance of believing communities and of personal commitments to Christ are benefits unforeseen a dozen years ago. Now they are a reality.

SOUL-TO-SOUL PAUCITY

The decline of transformative spiritual conversations in face-to-face encounters is compounded by the side effects of a plugged-in lifestyle. The addictive qualities of our devices have caused people to be uncomfortable around each other and incapable of meaningful conversation. These devices have created a need to more intentionally invest time and energy into building relationships with those we care for or are given charge to oversee in the integration of life and spiritual growth.

Without redeeming the use of technology toward sustaining the spiritual health of others, countless opportunities to connect more deeply with others are lost. Transparency, understanding, and empathy are minimized. Unanswered questions continue to abound, and those of a biblical or theological nature will contribute to one's spiritual illiteracy.

"Living the nightmare," is how one CEO describes the incidences of isolation, denial, and addictions that proliferate for men. The tendencies for women are to limit their sharing and not reveal their shortcomings in order to protect their image. These tendencies serve to perpetuate well-calculated distance between people. How much greater in our day, time, and culture is the need to have one "to whom you might make known your griefs, and by whom you might receive comfort from the Lord and encouragement in your Christian course."[10]

Without an available host on a chat during a streamed service, opportunities to further more personal connections can be lost. More tragic are the missed opportunities for viewers to come to faith and to advance that faith through an online format.

SOUL-TO-SOUL PREPARATION

The prevalence of technology in its many and ever-increasing modes can present a false sense of connection, a sense that somehow connections equal relationships and that many connections equal many relationships. With so many "relationships," does one need another? Be ready for some pushback. Some may argue that virtual conversations feel forced, that the length of time involved does not seem necessary, that the investment of time will come with minimal rewards, or that there is no perceivable way virtual conversations can go into depth. No one needs more to do, unless they can begin to be convinced of perceived or anticipated needs that can be met through conference and are willing to invest priceless time. Know that people are thirsty to talk with someone real who really cares.

When initial resistance is presented, receive it with patience. Carefully listen to these thoughts and validate the person by affirming that their concerns are heard. Most pushback is grounded on logistics. Limiting the size of a group is also important, to ensure a level of engagement that is substantive and transformative for all participants. Offer a trial period, during which tweaks can be made and after which the distance conference can be evaluated for its added value to the relationship.

Set up a time frame for these meetings that is neither too short nor too long, so that depth and engagement are both met. Whatever start and stop times are agreed upon, honor those. Be sensitive yet firm when establishing and maintaining boundaries for the sessions. If the group expects the conversation to last sixty minutes, give a kind warning that the time together will soon be coming to an end around the fifty-minute mark. Depending on the frequency of meetings, establishing trust and vulnerability may take two to six months before matters hidden in the recesses of a heart begin to be unveiled.

Technology continues to improve, but be aware that dropped calls and interference can still occur when using virtual platforms (such as Facebook, FaceTime, Zoom, Skype, Google Hangouts, and so on). Regardless of the format used for distance conferencing, pray ahead of time. Invite God's Spirit into the time to guide and allow all to listen and respond well, for His love to be extended wherever people are in their life journeys, and for the wisdom and humility to know what, when, and how to share and respond. When available, consider previous notes, written or mental; avoid going into a distance conference cold. Be mindful of matters that have the potential to distract or derail a conversation. Avoid multi-tasking, as one cannot truly concentrate well on more than one thing at a time. Stay focused to help you remain present in all conversations.

People need the space to be human and acceptance of whatever they bring to the conversation. Start each session with a welcome and assure participants of a safe and confidential place where trust is grown and rejection, condemnation, shaming, blame-shifting, and other con-versation stoppers will not be tolerated. Participants will not know the level of intimacy expected of themselves and others. How deep are we going to go? Will we have permission to be vague? Is it okay to be silent? Participants need thoughtful evidence that they are heard and validation that their thoughts are worthy of some form of interaction or affirmation. They want to know and be reminded that all are on the same team.

In the online context of a church, it is prudent to protect the pri-vacy of all viewers. Some conversations are better funneled outside the public chatroom into a more private one where contact information can be exchanged for prayer, counsel, and referrals.

Know that extending direct care to one person indirectly impacts another's understanding of that care, affirming the fact that the same care could be extended expectantly to them. This grows trust. One can feel cared for by observing how others were cared for. Virtual platforms can be effective tools for leveraging technology to extend direct and indirect care and concern through distance conferencing. Of course, letter-writing is still an option, a very fine option.

SOUL-TO-SOUL PROMPTS

Note: The following prompts could just as well be used in face-to-face conferences and show that little needs to be lost when conference is done at a distance.

Informational

1. The "one another" passages in God's Word were not limited to those in close proximity of each other, but would apply to those separated by distance. Which "one another" is given in these verses? Which ones surprised you? See Appendix 4.

2. In what ways have you observed or experienced God's kindness? Be specific.

3. Share a part of your life story where God's power, love, or forgiveness has grown your dependence on Him.

4. What have you observed in a prideful person?

5. What fear seems to keep lingering in your heart?

6. What spiritual conversations were involved in your process of coming to believe in Jesus?

7. Think of a time when a trial revealed your faith. What kind of faith did it reveal: inherited faith, shallow faith, conditional faith, or genuine faith?

Transitional

1. To which of the "one another's" is God seemingly attaching a person's name in your life? What is getting in the way of extending an attribute of God to this person?

2. Paul records in Romans 2:4 that God's kindness leads to repentance. How do you understand or experience this?

3. What was the basis of your resistance toward trusting and depending on God?

4. Pride is associated with prayerlessness, a lack of thankfulness. Backward-looking gratitude aids in combatting pride. Richard Baxter pens, "An unthankful person is but a devourer of mercies, and a grave to bury them in, and one that has not the wit or honesty to know and acknowledge the hand that gave them." How thankful a person are you?

5. If your God is small, you have every right to be given to disappointment, worry, doubt, and fear. But if your God is the One as revealed in His Word, you will not be overwhelmed or defeated by them. They will be met with the overarching knowledge that God is in control, and because He is love, He can only act in a loving way. John 6:20 states, "It is I. Don't be afraid." If He is who He says He is, if He is I Am, then the words *Don't be afraid* will begin to resonate with you. What truth about God is He proving to you that is aimed at your fear?

6. Gary McIntosh has observed that natural spiritual conversations with a family member or friend or staff member seem to be the most effective means in the process toward faith. "They want to feel that it's more natural—that we're just talking about life and sports and spiritual things. And through that conversation they come to understand what Christianity is and what commitment to Christ is, and some people just all of a sudden say, 'I believe.'"[11] Consider how a natural conversation might serve to draw attention to someone's own spiritual hunger and thirst.

7. Have you experienced a trial that drew you closer to God? What caused you to move closer to God instead of moving away from Him? How did He prove Himself faithful? Record these growth steps of faith in a journal.

Transformational

1. Pray for each other and each other's encounters with these ones, depending on the wisdom, strength, and courage to follow through with God's leading.

2. To whom is God leading you to extend kindness in His desire to draw them to Himself? What would that kindness look like?

3. What does your deepened dependence look like now?

4. What are you thankful for and how might this address a prideful tendency in you? Take time in prayer to thank God for the seen and unseen things in your life.

5. How are the words "It is I. Don't be afraid" beginning to resonate with you? Join another in prayer for God-given courage and grace to address the fear and allow the truth of who God is to take root.

6. To whom in your sphere of friendships is God leading you to have a natural spiritual conversation? Pray for God's timing, direction, and words.

7. What trial are you facing right now? Revisiting the reflections you recorded in your journal of God's past faithfulness, presence, and power, how can you begin to trust God again with your present challenge? Be specific.

PART III

SOUL-TO-SOUL BIBLE STUDIES: CONFERENCING THROUGH GOD'S WORD

The study of God's Word is necessary for transformation in a believer's life and for a thriving Christian community. The following Bible studies include prompts and questions that promote engagement, meditation, and conference. Each study includes these four parts: Ground Rules, Background, Ground Work, and Holy Ground.

GROUND RULES

Just as there are different types or genres of movies (sci-fi, comedy, crime, thriller, action, and so on), there are different types of literature or genres found in Scripture (Old Testament narratives, psalms, prophecy, Gospels, epistles, and so on). A key to plumbing the depths of God's Word is the ability to understand the genre of a particular passage. Each of the various genres of Scripture has unique characteristics and requires us to look through a different lens to be able to clearly focus on what God is showing us in a passage. As you apply the simple guidelines in each of the Bible studies, God will enlarge your understanding of Him through His Word.

BACKGROUND

Interpreting a passage requires a bit of investigative work. Sound interpretation requires an understanding of the historical context—the culture of the day, the religious atmosphere, Israel's fidelity (or infidelity, as was most often the case), and the intended audience. In addition, the literary context addresses issues about the author—the genre in which he chose to write, the big idea of a passage or paragraph, and the use of particular words.

The historical and cultural background information is important, and more important to the interpretation of some genres than others. Knowing the context of a passage from a gospel or an epistle, more so than for a psalm or proverb, is critical to the understanding of these. The cultural, social, and religious contexts of the time of the writing inform the meaning of the passage and need to be established before applying our own cultural, social, and religious contexts to the significance and application of the passage.

GROUND WORK

The questions and prompts for each of these passages are designed to engage the heart and soul of the disciple of Christ. They will move from informational to transitional to transformational types. As you move toward the transformational ones, the questions will become increasingly more thought-provoking and challenging, and will often require deep reflections and actions, both of which affect change in the heart. The goal is to involve our thought processes at a level that most deeply affects transformation.

HOLY GROUND

Holy ground is mentioned twice in the Bible, once in the Old Testament and once in the New Testament. Moses stands on holy ground (Exodus 3:5) and Stephen reminds his Jewish listeners of the holy ground on which Moses stood and spoke to God (Acts 7:33). It was not that the ground itself was holy but that it was rendered sacred by the presence of God, who is holy.

Wherever the Lord is constitutes holy ground. As the Lord abides in believers, as they are temples of His Holy Spirit, He is manifested in and through their lives. They represent Him as His ambassadors. Exhibiting and expressing God's kingdom reign is observed in a believer's godly character—how one thinks, responds, relates, and lives in our world. This requires the deepest kind of contemplation where a truth is imbedded so deeply in one's heart that it impacts what is thought, said, and done.

Various means of grace are interwoven in this portion of each study, so look for opportunities to accept God's invitations to learn more of Him, your relationship with Him, and yourself, and to cultivate empathy toward others through times of silence and solitude, fasting, prayer, confession, biblical hospitality, or biblical thanksgiving. (See Appendix 5). In addition, a necessary feature in these Bible studies is Conference.

Those who practice Conference can expect many benefits:

- Increased biblical literacy
- Time and space to distill God's truth for life

- Deepening of one's relationship with God
- Affirmation of a growing faith
- Deepening community
- Increased attentiveness to one another's souls
- Incorporation of other means of grace

Spiritual conversations that come from the study of God's Word help us to process and apply the truths God reveals about Himself, Jesus Christ, His kingdom, and the response He expects from us.

Our actions complete our knowledge. One's growth in Christlikeness will bear witness to God's truth imbedded in the heart and will manifest the truth of a Spirit-led life. This is the integration of faith in all facets and moments of life.

Each of the Bible studies on New Testament passages below has:

- Passage-specific prompts that will engage the disciple of Christ at increasingly challenging levels.
- Attention to the soul, remembering that the soul is both body and spirit (Genesis 2:7).
- Applications stemming from what is learned, as actions complete knowledge.
- A means of grace incorporated that allows for the truth of God's Word to nestle more deeply into the heart.
- Suggestions for conferencing with one another over discoveries from God's Word and how its truths impact the soul to a depth that fosters transformation.

Ready? Let's get started.

MATTHEW 1:1–16

Ground Rules

Matthew, Mark, Luke, and John comprise the four gospels. The word gospel means "good news," so the gospel of Matthew is the "good news" according to Matthew. The Gospels are biographical narratives or stories of Jesus's life, so we need to emphasize the broader context. Some historical and cultural background information is important. For example, some events in the first century, such as weddings, are quite different from those in the twenty-first. The focus of the Gospels is on Jesus, and they prove that he is the Messiah, the Christ, the Savior, the Anointed One, the long-awaited King, the One who was promised in the Old Testament and sent by God. He would come to establish God's kingdom and deliver mankind from their sins. Comparisons of the various gospels can be done since many of the same events and teachings appear in more than one gospel, but do so carefully. Focusing only on a particular gospel passage and its cross references in another gospel can lead to overlooking the purpose of the specific sequencing used by each gospel writer. The centrality of the kingdom of God necessitates reading the Gospels through that lens. The Gospels reveal who this King is, what He and His kingdom are like, and what kingdom citizens are to be like.

Background

The gospel according to Matthew was written by a Jewish tax collector whose name was changed from Levi to Matthew by Jesus. His name means "Gift of God." In his gospel, Matthew looked back to Hebrew prophecies as well as to Jesus's ministry and future plan for the church and His kingdom. There were few careers as despised as tax collecting in first century Judaism. Roman oppression of the Jewish people created an animosity toward Rome, so a Jewish tax collector collecting funds from the Jews for the Roman Empire constituted a collaborating traitor. In addition, tax collectors were given a fixed total of tax monies to collect. Anything over that amount could (and was) pocketed. Corruption was a reality. Imagine Matthew's predicament, especially as he records the "good news," possibly for Jewish Christians. Messiah has come, and He has come for all people. This is evident from the start, as Matthew begins his gospel record with a genealogy.

A genealogy. Must we begin with a genealogy? Surely there are more thought-provoking, soul-impacting passages to contemplate. Maybe. At first glance, this list consisting of three sets of fourteen generations could look like any other list of names, some familiar, most not. Matthew seems to emphasize a consistent theme in this genealogy, which aligns with his overall purpose for recording his gospel: to demonstrate the Messiahship of Jesus through God's faithfulness to His Abrahamic (Genesis 12:1–3) and Davidic (2 Samuel 7:12–16) covenants. While it might be easy to assume a self-righteous attitude toward Gentiles because a Jewish Messiah would be for the Jewish nation, Matthew's genealogy proves otherwise.

A closer look at this genealogy reveals a feature highly atypical for a Jewish genealogy: the names of women, five of them. It appears intentional that the names of four Old Testament women found in this patriarchal genealogy represent the expanse of Israel's history. Matthew departs from normal Jewish genealogical protocol in illustrating Gentiles as a crucial inclusion in Israel's history, where the righteousness or faith of these Gentile women proved a stark, sometimes embarrassing, contrast to that of the Israelites.

From the time of the patriarchs, Matthew records his first female entry: Tamar (v. 3). Her story is found in Genesis 38. She was a Canaanite woman (a non-Jew), widowed by the first two of three sons of Judah. Well aware of her father-in-law's unwillingness to give his third and last son to her, Tamar faces the reality of becoming a childless widow. She poses as a prostitute, lures Judah, becomes pregnant and bears twins. A definite highlight in anyone's family history, right? Yet Judah says of her, "She is more in the right than I" (Genesis 38:26), contrasting Judah's own wrongdoing in his withholding his third son from marrying her. Tamar is a recipient of God's over-riding faithfulness to preserve the line of the Messiah.

During the period of Conquest, we find Rahab (v. 5), Matthew's second female entry. Another Canaanite woman whose career choice and home in the red-light district of Jericho was well-known and well-visited. Her story is found in Joshua 2 and 6. Before chopping her off the proverbial family tree, note the evidence of her faith (Joshua 2:9, 11) based on what God had earlier said He would do (Exodus 15:15–16) and her inclusion into the heart of the Israelite community (Joshua 6:25). Rahab's believing faith allowed her to experience God's commitment to His people.

Might we see a reprieve in Matthew's third entry: Ruth (v. 5), the devoted daughter-in-law of Naomi? Perhaps. The four short chapters of the eighth book of the Bible reveal God's faithfulness to a discouraged

Israelite widow (and the nation) through a Moabitess. The author of the book of Ruth does not let the reader miss the fact that Ruth was a Moabitess, as he mentions it seven times in this short book. Matthew's audience would be reminded that Ruth was not of Israel. Her story took place during the period of the Judges. The very last verse of Judges summarizes the times of chaos and calamity: "In those days there was no king in Israel; everyone did whatever seemed right to him." (Judges 21:25). This period of Israel's history, characterized by disobedience and idol worship, represented days which Israel would want to forget, but Matthew does not allow it. Nor would he allow his readers to ignore Ruth's obedient faith.

Notice that Matthew only alludes to Bathsheba (v. 6) with a description of her as "Uriah's wife." She was King David's wife. But before that, she was Uriah the Hittite's. Before Matthew's audience could straighten their backs with pride, mindful of the glory days of their warrior-king of the United Kingdom, they would read the stinging reminder that this was David, Israel's most beloved king, in a period of his story marred by deception and premeditated murder. Contrast the loyal faith of Uriah, a Gentile warrior (2 Samuel 11–12). And when you consider Bathsheba's personal loss and suffering throughout her life, her bold faith comes to the fore.

Mary understood her lowly and humble estate. She also understood Joseph's concern over the growing profile of her pregnancy and the reality of ridicule and shame, but she chose to believe and trust God's plan for her, Israel, and the world. She treasured and meditated on the events of Jesus's birth and life while recognizing her need for deliverance from sin and guilt and magnifying her Lord. She stood in silence by the cross witnessing the agony of blasphemes and the crucifixion of the One she birthed. Her obedient faith is found in a magnificent God.

Four Old Testament women, some of questionable repute, who demonstrated unquestionable faith or devotion against a backdrop of Israel's past that should have been, by all accounts, historical highlights. Along with Mary, each one is intentionally included in a Jewish genealogy; the genealogy uniquely belonging to Jesus the Messiah. Faith and obedience move beyond ethnic boundaries. And so would the gospel message. There would be no room for ethnic pride when it came to matters of the Messiah. The King of the Jews came for the world. His kingdom would be all-inclusive. Matthew 28:18–20, at the close of Matthew's gospel, proves it again.

A genealogy begins the "good news" according to Matthew. Can you think of a better way for the New Testament to start?

Ground Work

- Pray a prayer of readiness and openness to God. Read Matthew 1:1–16 twice through. Record any thoughts that come to mind.
- From the genealogy, which names are familiar to you?
- Read the passage again aloud. Choose one (or more) of the four Old Testament women and read their stories. Their references are given.

  - Tamar (Genesis 38:1–30): Who are the characters involved in this story? Step into Tamar's sandals. What thoughts and emotions might you have?
  - Rahab (Joshua 2; Joshua 6): When you get to Joshua 2:9, look up these cross references: Exodus 23:27 and Deuteronomy 2:25. What event occurred between the writing of Exodus and Deuteronomy? What does God reveal about Himself? Step into Rahab's sandals. What thoughts and emotions might you have?
  - Ruth (Read the 4 short chapters of this book): This book is really about the relationship between God and Naomi. She had every right to be discouraged and bitter. Yet, God surrounds her with His faithful loving-kindness (*hesed*). Through that lens, what does God reveal about Himself and how He relates to people, no matter what emotional state they may be experiencing? What does God reveal about Himself? Step into Naomi's sandals. What thoughts and emotions might you have?
  - Wife of Uriah (2 Samuel 11:1–12:25): Who are the characters involved in this story? What does God reveal about Himself? Step into David's sandals and then step into Nathan's. What thoughts and emotions might you have?

- Why is it important that He is the head of the church (Colossians 1:18) and His church is to be for all people?
- How is the purpose of Matthew's gospel echoed in the closing verses (Matthew 28:18–20) of the book?

Holy Ground

- What attribute of God have you found revealed in the dynamics of God's relationship with these women or with Israel in preserving the Messianic line? What new insight do you have about God's Kingdom? Incorporate that aspect into prayer.
- Conference with a trusted friend to share what attitude or action hinders you from seeing, or helps you to see, the all-inclusiveness of the gospel. Are there some people or people groups that you would rather objectify and marginalize than to see them as made in the image of God and in need of knowing Him? Be honest.
- In what way might you depend on God's Spirit to reflect or express His desire for someone to know the inclusiveness of His kingdom? This may begin with exercising biblical hospitality, extending friendship to a stranger. Would you allow God to direct you to this person? Will you, as you lean on His Spirit for guidance and courage, respond in obedience? Be specific.
- Reread the passage. Spend some time alone reflecting on your recorded thoughts and how God has spoken to your soul through His Word. As you have more of God's character, identify some praise-worthy descriptors for God and then do just that: praise Him.

MATTHEW 12:29–32; MATTHEW 13:22–32

Ground Rules

Matthew, Mark, Luke, and John comprise the four gospels. The word gospel means "good news," so the gospel of Matthew is the "good news" according to Matthew. The Gospels are biographical narratives or stories of Jesus's life, so we need to emphasize the broader context. Some historical and cultural background information is important. For example, some events in the first century, such as weddings, are quite different from those in the twenty-first. The focus of the Gospels is on Jesus, and they prove that He is the Messiah, the Christ, the Savior, the Anointed One, the long-awaited King, the One who was promised in the Old Testament and sent by God. He would come to establish God's kingdom and deliver mankind from their sins. Comparisons of the various gospels can be done since many of the same events and teachings appear in more than one gospel, but do so carefully. Focusing only on a particular gospel passage and its cross references in another gospel can lead to overlooking the original purpose of the specific sequencing used by each gospel writer. The centrality of the kingdom of God necessitates reading the gospels through that lens. The Gospels reveal who this King is, what He and His kingdom are like and what kingdom citizens are to be like.

Background

Matthew presents Jesus as the Messiah in the first four chapters of his gospel. After giving testament to Jesus's words (Chapters 5–7) and His confirming works (Chapters 8–10), Matthew goes on to record the progressively confrontational opposition toward Jesus. Jesus's ministry was always plagued with antagonists. In this portion of Matthew's gospel, the religious leaders who represent the nation reject Jesus as the Messiah. Meet the Pharisees.

The intertestamental time was the period of about four hundred years between the Old and New Testament events. Though characterized by the silence of God, Israel was rich with history. The group known as the Pharisees originated during this time. They were most influential among the common people, being highly regarded, respected, and admired as spiritual leaders. In the synagogues ("a gathering together") the people would meet to hear the Law and the Prophets read and preached, as interpreted and expounded by the Pharisees.

The Pharisees were focused on God and His Word and were devoted to being obedient to it and living it out. They were godly people who sought to honor God by keeping the Law. Their pursuit of obedience, however, involved implementing numerous supplementary regulations intended to protect the Law, forming a "fence" or "guardrail" around the Law. Adherence to what would eventually become 613 various directives was required to keep people from disobeying the Law. Tradition had become Scripture. This effectively fenced off many people from the life of the synagogue, creating a chasm between those who were part of the Pharisaic brotherhood and those "sinners" who were not diligent enough to keep the plethora of rules.

Jesus defied the Pharisees' interpretation of the Law. In God's eyes, righteousness was a matter of the heart and was not contingent upon the strict adherence to their interpretation of the rules. In the eyes of the Pharisees, Jesus was sabotaging their efforts. The Pharisees were steeped in frustration and sought to trap Jesus with His own words and even plot His murder.

It is not difficult to see the potential and understand the actual reasons behind the confrontations Jesus and the Pharisees would have. After all, they were the ones who knew the Law and, while embracing a messianic hope, had longed to see the coming Kingdom of God. They were the experts in knowing the God of the Israelites. If anyone should have been able to recognize the Messiah when he arrived, it should have been them.

Yet when they come face to face with Jesus, the incarnate God, the God-man, and observe firsthand His miracles, they attribute the power and intent to the Evil One. What should have been a welcomed reception was instead a hostile rejection. Their progressive antagonism and ultimate rejection of Jesus came to a defining moment, climaxed by the miraculous healing of the demonized blind mute. As representative of the entire nation, the religious leaders now rejected Jesus as the Messiah and their rejection became the pivotal moment in Jesus's teaching on the kingdom of God. Jesus began to teach using parables. Those who had ears to hear and hearts to know God would understand him; those who didn't, wouldn't. The first parable Jesus taught is the entry point for determining if one has a heart for God's kingdom.

MATTHEW 13:1–23

It is not uncommon to hear a parable described as "an earthly story with a heavenly meaning." While that may be true, the purposeful intention of a parable can be easily lost. Jesus usually used parables to give His listeners a picture of the King, His Kingdom, or of values held by the King. In and through parables, Jesus pushes the envelope. His parables demand a response. This parable in Matthew 13, recorded in the synoptic gospels (Matthew, Mark, and Luke) clearly demonstrates this.

Jesus's listeners would be very familiar with stories that used agriculture or farming language. This familiar parable describes four different types of soil and the plants whose purpose is to bear fruit. Jesus uses this soil to present four different types of receptive hearts. Three lack the ability to be fruitful. One is God-pleasing. Listeners would easily identify with the objects of Jesus's illustration: road, rocks, soil, weeds, and crops.

The trodden road pictures impenetrable hearts, never giving God a real chance. The choking rocks depict the cosmetic, fair-weathered heart. When the going gets tough, they're gone. The asphyxiating weeds portray the heart entangled in the things of the world. The things of God take a backseat. The fertile soil epitomized the heart of a life available to and effective for God's kingdom.

Jesus encountered all these types of hearts in

The Pharisees	John 3:1–2, 12:42, 19:38–40;
	Philippians 3:4–6
Some disciples	John 6:52–66
A rich young ruler	Luke 18:18–30
The Samaritan woman	John 4:1–42

It is easy enough to pick out the soil of choice; it is equally easy to pick out the heart of choice. But this parable was the first of Jesus's recorded by Matthew. He knew it was important to assess the receptivity of one's own heart. If your heart is receptive to the things of God, then you would understand what was to come. But if your heart is not receptive to the things of God, nothing of the rest of what Jesus would teach and do would make much sense. This parable presents a matter of conviction. Jesus pushes the envelope. The first century listener would have heard, "Which type of soil are you?" "How receptive a heart do you have for God and His kingdom?" The twenty-first century listener must hear the same questions and give an honest answer to the Sower.

Ground Work

- Pray for a readiness and openness to God. Read Matthew 12:29–32 and Matthew 13:22–32 a couple of times through. Record any thoughts that come to mind.

- Some believers are troubled as they ponder Jesus's words regarding the blasphemy of the Holy Spirit, fearing they've committed the unforgiveable or unpardonable sin. Here, the Pharisees have attributed Jesus's act of casting out a demon to Satan, God's enemy, and have denied that Jesus's miracles are done by the power of God's Spirit. The unpardonable sin is when a person consciously, willfully, and consistently rejects the work of the Spirit. It is the Spirit who bears witness to the reality of Jesus as the Savior to receive the forgiveness that leads to salvation. The Pharisees' hearts are hard, and they do not recognize their own need. God's offer of mercy is refused. For a believer, that mercy is humbly accepted. This is then translated into a transforming life made possible by God alone. Have you struggled with trusting that you are a child of God? How will you let the truth of Romans 8:16 become a reality?

- Read the passage aloud. Considering the status and role of a Pharisee, how likely is it that you would have been one?

- Choose any of the four examples given of those whom Jesus encountered. Record their response or lack of response. With whose heart response do you most resonate? Be a little surprised. Incorporate that aspect into prayer.

- Matthew records his gospel to show that Jesus is the Messiah. From this passage, what do you glean about this Messiah? The most important question each one of us must answer is, "Who do you say Jesus is?" Record your personal response.

Holy Ground

- Reread the passage. Spend time alone with God with a brief fast. Try fasting for one hour before advancing to a typical fast, which is twenty-four hours. Stay hydrated while removing food and all forms of technology that interfere with sensing His presence and hearing His voice. After the noises of the world have sufficiently been silenced, ask Him to reveal some fears you have. Fasting before God reveals our fears; our fears reveal our idols. The attitudes or actions hindering you from having the choicest of receptive hearts can be linked to your fears and idols. Allow yourself to begin to give these to Jesus, the only one who really wants and can do something about them for you.

What relationship is there between your dependence on technology and your dependence on God?

How is God stirring in you to cultivate a more receptive heart?

Identify the most prominent fear you have. What idol is associated with that fear?

- ◉ Conference with a trusted friend to share:
- ◉ Your takeaways from your fast.
- ◉ What has been resonating in your heart and soul in response to the above prompts on fears and idols.
- ◉ How you can allow yourself to present those idols to God in order for Him to do a greater work in you.

• Reread the passage. Spend some time alone reflecting on your recorded thoughts and the experience of sharing those thoughts. How has God spoken to you through His Word, His Spirit, and His community?

JOHN 15:1–12

Ground Rules

Matthew, Mark, Luke, and John comprise the four gospels. The word gospel means "good news," so the gospel of John is the "good news" according to John. The Gospels are biographical narratives or stories of Jesus's life, so we need to emphasize the broader context. Some historical and cultural background information is important. For example, some events in the first century, such as weddings, are quite different from those in the twenty-first. The focus of the Gospels is on Jesus, and they prove that he is the Messiah, the Christ, the Savior, the Anointed One, the long-awaited King, the One who was promised in the Old Testament and sent by God. He would come to establish God's kingdom and deliver mankind from their sins. Comparisons of the various gospels can be done since many of the same events and teachings appear in more than one gospel, but do so carefully. Focusing only on a particular gospel passage and its cross references in another gospel can lead to overlooking the original purpose of the specific sequencing used by each gospel writer. The centrality of the kingdom of God necessitates reading the gospels through that lens. The Gospels reveal who this King is, what He and His kingdom are like and what kingdom citizens are to be like.

Background

Only Matthew and John were written by eyewitnesses of Jesus's earthly ministry. John identifies himself in his gospel as "the one Jesus loved" (John 13:23, 20:2, 21:7). Whereas Matthew, Mark, and Luke were written earlier in the first century, John's gospel is written later, c. AD 80–90. Having written his gospel toward the latter part of the first century, John does not include much of the material found in Matthew, Mark, and Luke—the Synoptic Gospels—yet he includes material not found there. Almost 50 percent of John's gospel focuses on the last week of Jesus's life. In fact, John emphasizes Jesus's resurrection more than the other three Gospels combined.

A comprehensive reading of John's gospel reveals his use of many opposites: light and darkness, from above and from below, truth and lie, sight and blindness, life and death, faith and unbelief. You will also find these words often: "believe" (sixty times) and "eternal life" (sixteen times). The reader's response to God and His kingdom is found only in the crucified, risen, and ascended Messiah, Jesus Christ. The purpose for John recording his gospel can be found in John 20:30–31: "But these are written so that you may believe Jesus is the Messiah, the Son of God, and by believing you may have life in His name." One can now more easily understand why the gospel of John is often called the "Gospel of decision."

Giving witness to the truth of Jesus's identity is critical for others coming to faith in Him. As part of His farewell discourse, Jesus speaks words of particular importance. In a matter of hours He would be arrested, wrongly accused, illegally judged, taunted and mocked, mercilessly flogged, and sentenced to death by crucifixion with hands and feet nailed to a Roman cross. His words would be particularly weighty.

In this passage you will be exploring, Jesus uses an extended metaphor of the vine and the branches, giving an interpretation and application afterward. Jesus's use of vine imagery was not only familiar to His followers because of their agrarian culture, but vines appeared in the temple. A first-century Jewish historian, Josephus, noted that above a linen curtain of purple, scarlet, and blue flowers was a gigantic grapevine made of pure gold. Wealthy citizens could bring gifts of gold tendrils, grapes, or leaves to be added by metal workers to the ever-growing vine. This fruitful vine represented Israel (*Ant.* 15.395), planted and tended to by God. In all the Old Testament contexts where "vine" is used (Hosea 10:1–2; Isaiah 5:1–7; Jeremiah 2:21; Ezekiel 15:1–5, 17:1–21, 19:10–14; Psalm 80:8–18), all speak of Israel. The nation is described as having great potential, but due to its moral and spiritual failure, Israel is chastised for not bearing fruit.

Jesus states, "I am the true vine" (15:1). This is Jesus's final "I am" statement. In contrast to the Old Testament vine metaphors, all of which refer to Israel, the true vine will bear fruit. Fruit-bearing is the evidence of attachment to the vine. The key word in this passage is "remaining" or "abiding." Notice that the charge is not to bear fruit but to abide.

The joy in John 15:11 matches the peace promised in John 14:27. Jesus desires that His joy would be in His disciples. Jesus's joy has come through His reliance on God the Father and His obedience to God's will. As followers of Christ, we inherit Jesus's joy and the Spirit-given capacity to enjoy God in the same manner—by trusting and obeying.

Having described the life-giving vine and our need to share in His life and love in order to live, Jesus now describes life among the branches. In verse 12, he repeats His command to love one another (John 13:34). This love is an outgrowth of a life that has witnessed the dramatic quality of God's love (John 15:13) when His Son died on behalf of those He loves. This love is directed to others and to God. Jesus now calls His disciples "friends," and what characterizes such friends is their obedience to Jesus. Being called a friend of God is the highest relationship possible between God and a human being. Jesus has chosen believers as friends, and in Facebook language, He will never delete or "unfollow" you. As friends of God, disciples of Jesus possess God's Word because of the Spirit (John 14:25–26), and receive ongoing revelations of Jesus (John 16:12–13). Therefore, God's heart can be known to His children and thus we become participants in what God is doing. Our prayers reflect His desires. This will be particularly important as Jesus continues with His explanation of the hatred of the world toward Him and those who choose to follow Him.

Ground Work

- Pray for a readiness and openness to God. Read John 15:1–12 a couple of times through. Record any thoughts that come to mind.
- The theme of abundance is clearly found throughout John's gospel. Look at Amos 9:13–14 as you think of the water Jesus turned to wine at Cana and all 120–180 gallons of bread and fish that fed over five thousand people! Jesus brought the expected messianic abundance in fulfillment of the Old Testament. Messianic expectations are what the Jewish people had in anticipation of God sending the One who would save them. When the Messiah came and ushered in His kingdom, the lame would leap (5:1–9; and Isaiah 35:6) and the blind would see (9:1–7 and Isaiah 35:5). He would be the "good Shepherd," in contrast to the bad shepherds who led Israel (10:11 and Ezekiel 34), and He would be the "true vine" (15:1) in contrast to the wretched and degenerate vine (Isaiah 5:7 and Jeremiah 2:21).

  In God's kingdom is abundance, yet it is squandered by Israel's leaders. Look at Ezekiel 34 and a few of the verses surrounding Isaiah 5:7 and Jeremiah 2:21. What did this squandering look like? What might it look like in your life?
- Notice that the command to "remain" or "abide" is repeated ten times in these twelve verses. The disciples' salvation is not in question; the focus is living the words of Jesus as one is in union with Him. The disciple must remain in Christ.

  What do these aspects of "remaining in Christ" look like in your life? How do you bear the witness of God the Father, Jesus the Son, and God's Holy Spirit abiding in you, especially in challenging

circumstances? Be specific, remembering that obeying His words
is a demonstration of trusting in His love and loving ways.

- ⊚ Living out His words in your life (v. 7):
- ⊚ Obedience (v. 10):
- ⊚ Love (v. 12):

What are the results of remaining/abiding? What evidence of
the following is seen and experienced in your life?

- ⊚ To bear _____. What is the "fruit"? (vv. 2, 5, 8,
  and 16)
- ⊚ Answered _____ (vv. 7 and 16)
- ⊚ _____ given to the Father (v. 8)
- ⊚ Perfect _____ (v. 11)

How might a Christian miss out on God's intent if this command is misinterpreted to suggest that one is to bear fruit versus
abide?

- Here are a few references to the Person of the Holy Spirit. What do
  each say about the third Person of the Trinity?
  - ⊚ Romans 8:16
  - ⊚ Romans 8:26–27
  - ⊚ Romans 8:28
  - ⊚ 2 Corinthians 3:6
  - ⊚ Ephesians 3:16
  - ⊚ Ephesians 4:30
  - ⊚ Galatians 5:18
  - ⊚ Romans 8:14

Holy Ground

- Remain in Me, and I in you. Seven words that should impact
  everything we think, do, and say.
  - ⊚ What does this "remaining" or "abiding" look like in
    your life? Be specific.
  - ⊚ What difference would your remaining in Christ make in
    your life?

If this sounds like a huge undertaking, it is. That is why God's
giving of His Spirit is so necessary. The first of three promises of

the Holy Spirit is given in John 14:12–17. The second appears in John 14:25–31. Jesus teaches in metaphorical language of the vine and the branches in John 15:1–17 and forewarns His disciples of expected conflict with the world in John 15:18–25, before giving the third of three promises of the Holy Spirit in John 15:26–16:4a.

Spend an hour with God alone. Remove yourself from the constant busyness and the unrelenting demands to which you have grown accustomed. In your time of silence and solitude, ponder how you can begin or continue your soul's reliance on God's Spirit for the challenge you identified above. Be specific.

- Jesus's command is to love one another as He has loved you (v. 12). John 15:12–17 explains it with more detail. To love sacrificially is to hand over one's own life for others—just as Jesus did on the cross. The first use of the word "love" in the Bible is found in Genesis 22:2, where God tests Abraham, "'Take your son,' he said, 'your only son Isaac, whom you *love*, go to the land of Moriah, and offer him there as a burnt offering on one of the mountains I will tell you about.'" So God defines love, from the very beginning, as a father's willingness to sacrifice his son and the son's willingness to be sacrificed. How does God's definition of love compare to the world's, which focuses on self and selfish desires? How does God's definition of love alter and impact your understanding of love?

In His infinite love, God sends Jesus and now He sends you and me as His witnesses. The word "witness" is found fourteen times as a noun and thirty-three times as a verb in John's gospel. Jesus's life of integrity through His "show and tell" is how His disciples, then and now, are to bear witness of their own growing dependence on the Spirit. To what is your life bearing witness? If not God's Spirit, then what?

- Conference with a trusted friend to
    - ◉ Share your takeaways from your time alone with God in silence and solitude.
    - ◉ Discover how you can let God's Spirit have more of His way in your life? Be specific.
    - ◉ Share the name of the person God is bringing to your

attention—someone needing to know and experience
Jesus's love through your unique "show and tell." How
will that be approached? Be specific.

PHILIPPIANS 4:1-3

Ground Rules

Twenty-one of the twenty-seven books of the New Testament are epistles
or letters. If an apostle or another leader could not be physically present
to address a church situation, the next best option was to write a letter and
send it by personal courier. These written words carried the same authoritative weight as would the words spoken by the writer himself. Letters
were occasional—not that they were randomly or sporadically written—
but they addressed a specific occasion or state of affairs. A behavior
needing correcting (1 Corinthians 5:1-5, an incestuous man), a doctrinal
error needing to be set right (Galatians 2:14, certain Jewish Christians
[Judaizers] convincing Gentiles to observe Jewish religious customs, to
"live like Jews"), or a misunderstanding (1 Thessalonians 4:16, confusion
over "the dead in Christ").

A trained scribe or secretary (*amanuensis*) typically wrote a letter for
the author. As there was no postal service, the finished copy would be
hand delivered by a trusted individual, who could also answer questions
to ensure a correct understanding of the letter. An epistle was meant to be
read aloud again and again, not least because literacy was so low.

All of the epistles were written in the first century and follow the
conventional format of a first century letter: the greeting, the body of the
letter, and its conclusion. The greeting includes the name of the writer,
name of the recipients, and an introductory opening prayer. Where this
is missing, pay attention, because it means there is a serious matter about
to be addressed. The body of a letter addresses the specific situation. And
the letter ends with a closing grace benediction. Each epistle falls into one
of two categories: Pauline, written by the apostle Paul and named after
the recipients, and General or catholic, written by others and, excepting
Hebrews, named after the non-Pauline authors.

As one would do today with an email or text message, read the whole of the letter in one sitting. This allows for the author's argument to be traced and better understood. You will find that the paragraphs make up the units of thought, not individual verses. Even as a whole, we still only understand half of the conversation, much like hearing one side of a phone conversation. This is where historical context comes in. Knowing what was going on when and with whom is critical for reading and interpreting an epistle. Along with reading these letters historically, we can read them theologically, discovering what God reveals about Himself.

When reading any part of Scripture, the meaning of a passage is what the original author intended his audience to know and understand. This is especially important when reading and interpreting the epistles because the epistle writer had a specific desired outcome for the reader(s) in response to his letter. Present-day implications and application should still be aligned with the author's intent.

Background

Paul established the church in Philippi in AD 51 during his second of three missionary journeys in response to the God-given Macedonian vision (Acts 16:9–10). This church was the first European church and was closer to Paul than any of his other church plants. This warmly written, upbeat letter was penned while Paul was in prison and is one of four "prison" epistles (Ephesians, Philippians, Colossians, and Philemon). Paul thanks the Philippian church for the encouragement and financial support sent through Epaphroditus. Amid the afflictions and sufferings experienced by Paul and the threat of division in the church, the themes of joy and unity in this letter are strong.

Paul presents reasons for unity throughout the entire letter. And in almost stealthlike manner, toward the end of the letter, Paul devotes three of the letter's 104 verses (4:1–3), to carefully, pastorally, and respectfully mention the personal conflict that was threatening the unity of the church. Jesus continues to be magnified in and through Paul's imprisonment, and would be glorified in the resolution of this conflict. Instead of having prideful hearts that cause quarreling and conflict, the Philippian believers were challenged to know and exhibit the mind and humility of Christ.

Ground Work

- Read Acts 16:11–15 and describe Lydia, the first convert, and the human and divine involved in her conversion. Lydia's name implies a servant or slave background, but her status implies a single, freed woman of significant means.
- Read Paul's entire letter to the Philippian church through the lens of joy and unity. Record your observations.
- Reread Philippians 4:1–3. Euodia and Syntyche[1] were coworkers alongside Paul in the work of the gospel. Both likely enjoyed the camaraderie not unlike that which Timothy and Epaphroditus (Chapter 3) experienced with Paul. Perhaps as co-laborers with Paul, they had enjoyed sweet fellowship as close friends, coworkers, and leaders in the community. Paul saw the like-mindedness they enjoyed and experienced, but something was awry. Coworkers had become rivals. Disharmony existed, in response to which Paul addresses not the issue but those involved.

Had these leaders grown accustomed to having things done their own way? When did competition, rivalry, and selfish ambition set in? How did each become more concerned with their own interests than those of others? When did self-importance start destroying a friendship? Did they stop affirming or encouraging each other?

Unresolved conflict is not typically confined to a single conversation or encounter between two people. To the contrary, each party feels the need to garner support, forcing unsuspecting members of the community to "choose sides." The one with the most, or at least the most powerful, players, wins. Both sides jockey for the upper hand. Disharmony flourishes and unity is threatened. Unity is a theme of this letter because it was threatened in this church.

In light of unresolved conflict that threatened this community, Paul neither takes sides nor does he encourage others to do so. Instead, he enlists the help of one or perhaps others to come alongside and help. The Philippian listeners were charged to strive together for the faith of the gospel. It would take commitment and work. Unity, though a gift to the Church, is not kept without effort, hard effort. Paul enlists the help of true friends, fellow workers.

He appeals on a corporate level to bring opposing sides together. Community efforts can diffuse the antagonism and resentment between individuals.

- What would the community hear again and again in this letter?
  - Philippians 1:27
  - Philippians 2:2–8
  - Philippians 2:14–15
  - Philippians 4:2–5
- What was the Philippian community to remember?
  - Philippians 1:7–11
  - Philippians 2:1–4
  - Philippians 2:13
  - Philippians 3:13 and 20
- Philippians 4:1 begins with a "So then." What is it there for?
- Paul needed the community to understand what was at stake. It was more than the elements of a quarrel between two people. At issue was the gospel in Philippi. The gospel was at stake. The gospel was and is always at stake. The gospel message of forgiveness and reconciliation was threatened. How would the world know and understand the God of forgiveness and reconciliation if His own people lived unreconciled toward each other?
- Reread the entire letter through the lens of Paul desiring the Philippians to individually exercise Christlike humility toward unity for the corporate body. Note your observations.
- Improper thoughts can rob us of God's peace in our lives. How have you experienced this truth?

    How can meditating on whatever is "true, honorable, just, pure, lovely, commendable, morally excellent, and praiseworthy" (Philippians 4:8) change a condemning or hurtful attitude in one who knows and experiences God's stabilizing, ever-available peace?

Holy Ground

- Conflict. Major offensives over minor offenses. Mountain reactions over molehill reasons, though they did not seem like molehills at the time. No matter how many times we enjoy and celebrate the teamwork and solidarity of working alongside others, the occurrence of conflict is a reality. Not all conflict is bad, however. Many new ideas and creative methods have come out of conflict. But when the dark side of conflict goes unresolved, symptoms manifest. Though unresolved conflict may be silently and internally harbored, it will eventually exhibit external symptoms. Its self-destructiveness reaches depths where even a fleeting glimpse of an offender or the mention of their name triggers a change in demeanor and disposition. We rationalize—"rational lies"—to justify our must-win anger, attitudes, or actions. Bitterness and anger are slow, sure, and systemic. Reliving arguments and reinforcing our defense come at a cost. The loss of sleep, time, attention, health, a desire to reconcile, a clear conscience, and a relationship seem an acceptable sacrifice for the satisfaction of the "must-win."

Spend thirty minutes alone with God to consider your responses to these prompts.

- Can you affirm that God has all authority in your life?
- Can you affirm that God is all powerful?
- Identify a relationship or lack of relationship of yours that most closely fits the above description.
- What reservations do you have in seeking reconciliation with this person? Pen those reservations here.

As a prelude to reconciliation, there is forgiveness. Forgiveness involves you choosing to let go of past hurts that negatively impact our present and future decisions and actions. Reconciliation can come in many forms. To forgive and to be reconciled does not mean the offense or the offender was right. Forgiveness on our part allows us to move forward, trusting God for His justice instead of devising plans for vengeance.

- Will you be found obedient when God presents you with the opportunity to depend on Him for the attitude and words to seek forgiveness and reconciliation? Be careful here. If you respond with, "I can't," you are denying God's power. If you respond with, "I won't," you are denying God's authority. Compare this to how you answered the first prompt in this Holy Ground section. The process of growing more dependent on His Spirit gives increasing evidence of the lordship of Christ in your life, as we are called to "shine like stars" (Philippians 2:15). Write your response here. Be specific.

• Conference with a trusted friend to share what has been resonating or wrestling in your heart and soul.

COLOSSIANS 3:1–17

Ground Rules

Twenty-one of the twenty-seven books of the New Testament are epistles or letters. If an apostle or another leader could not be physically present to address a church situation, the next best option was to write a letter and send it by personal courier. These written words carried the same authoritative weight as would the words spoken by the writer himself. Letters were occasional—not that these were randomly or sporadically written—but addressed a specific occasion or state of affairs. A behavior needing correcting (1 Corinthians 5:1–5, an incestuous man), a doctrinal error needing to be set right (Galatians 2:14, certain Jewish Christians [Judaizers] convincing Gentiles to observe Jewish religious customs, to "live like Jews"), or a misunderstanding (1 Thessalonians 4:16, confusion over "the dead in Christ").

A trained scribe or secretary (*amanuensis*) typically wrote a letter for the author of that letter. As there was no postal service, the finished copy would be hand delivered by a trusted individual, who could also answer questions to ensure a correct understanding of the letter. An epistle was meant to be read aloud again and again, not least because literacy was so low.

All of the epistles were written in the first century and follow the conventional format of a first century letter: the greeting, the body of the letter, and its conclusion. The greeting includes the name of the writer, name of the recipients, and an introductory opening prayer. Where this is missing, pay attention, because it means there is a serious matter about to be addressed. The body of a letter addresses the specific situation. And the letter ends with a closing grace benediction. Each epistle falls into one of two categories: Pauline, written by the apostle Paul and named after the recipients, and General or catholic, whose titles, except Hebrews, were the names of the non-Pauline authors.

As one would do today with an email or text message, read the whole of the letter in one sitting. This allows for the author's argument to be traced and better understood. You will find that the paragraphs make up the units of thought, not individual verses. Even as a whole, we still only understand half of the conversation, much like hearing one side of a phone conversation. This is where historical context comes in. Knowing what was going on when and with whom is most critical for reading and interpreting an epistle. Along with reading these letters historically, we can read them theologically, discovering what God reveals about Himself.

When reading any part of Scripture, the meaning of a passage is what the original author intended his audience to know and understand. This is especially important when reading and interpreting the epistles because the epistle writer had a specific desired outcome for the reader(s) in response to his letter. Present-day implications and application should still be aligned with the author's intent.

Background

The letter to the saints of the Colossian church was written by Paul (with Timothy) while in a Roman prison. This letter is one of four known as the "prison" epistles: Ephesians, Philippians, Colossians, and Philemon. This church was planted by a new believer while Paul was in Ephesus, so he had not ever visited it in person. Nevertheless, his deep love for the Christ followers in Colossae caused him concern as theologically errant teaching had infiltrated the church.

There is no firm consensus on what this empty and deceitful "philosophy" (Colossians 2:8) was that Paul warns against. At the very least, it could have been a blending of a number of religious ideas (or syncretism), whose practices included angel worship and the wearing of amulets or charms with names of angels or spirits on them meant to protect the wearer. Some restrictions were also required that Paul describes as "severe treatment of the body" (Colossians 2:23). What is certain, though, is that the philosophy was not aligned with the truth of the person of Jesus Christ. Of the letter's ninety-five verses, almost half mention or make reference to Jesus Christ.

The letter begins with Paul thanking the Colossians and reminding them of his prayers for them. His updates include a report of the gospel spreading to the farthest parts of the Roman empire. He then extols the surpassing greatness of Christ as the exact image of the invisible God, Creator and Sustainer over all creation, head of the Church, and upholds His completed work on the cross (Colossians 1:15–20). Paul's authoritative words remind the Colossian believers of Jesus's power and authority. Then he presents the mystery: God has come down, and Christ has come in (Colossians 1:27).

Following Paul's argument, he then reminds the Colossian readers that because Jesus is Lord, believers are now found in Him; they are in Christ (Colossians 2:7, 10–13). This knowledge would not only be the antidote against succumbing to the false teaching infiltrating the hearts of believers, but also their new nature would manifest in observable differences. Paul is adamant that his readers see the futility of the errant philosophy and the truth of new life in Christ. If his readers are deceived by this false teaching, they would lack the knowledge of who Jesus is and therefore lack the knowledge of who they are in Him and the ability to live out that truth. Ultimately, they would be unable to join Paul in his work of reaching others for Christ and many would remain lost. The gospel was at stake.

Ground Work

- Read the entire letter to the church in Colossae. Record your thoughts here.
- In today's world, the word "meditation" conjures up a wide variety of thoughts and reservations. If you've ever worried about anything, you've meditated. Biblical meditation is powerful and effective in embedding God's Word more deeply into our hearts. Ruminating on biblical truths allows us to carry these truths wherever we go and affects everything we think, do, and say. As we understand conference to be those conversations

where biblical truths and soul care come together, meditation, as the Puritans understood it, was considered conference within ourselves.

Reread Colossians 3:1–17. Meditate on these words of life.

- ⊚ After describing God's work in us through Christ and God's victory over opposing forces through the completed work of Christ on the cross (1:13, 20), Paul lists the five ways one denies the holiness of God in verse 5. Describe how each is a form of idolatry.

Which one(s) continue to be a struggle in which God is wanting and equipping you to surrender more fully to Him?

- ⊚ List the five ways one denies God's plan for community in verse 8. Describe how each hinders participation in a loving and united community.

Which one(s) continue to be a struggle in which God is wanting and equipping you to surrender more fully to Him?

- ⊚ What does it mean to "put on the new self" (v. 10)? List the five characteristics a Christ follower, because he or she is chosen and holy and dearly loved, is to put on in verse 12. What is the basis for these actions? Describe how each virtue is a way of responding to God's grace.

How will you let your response to God's grace impact the struggles you identified above?

- In Colossians 3:13, Paul describes how the above virtues build a community. The Christian is characterized by "bearing with one another and forgiving one another." To live out forgiveness is to live out the gospel—God's forgiveness toward us in Jesus's death on the cross. On what basis is a Christian able to forgive anyone?
- Three times in Colossians 3:15–17, a form of the word "thanks" appears. In each, gratitude is directed to God, but the words also point to the basis for giving thanks. How do each of these verses show that?
  - ⊚ v. 15
  - ⊚ v. 16
  - ⊚ v. 17

- Read and reflect on these words from an English puritan, George Swinnock:

> Meditate upon his mercies to you from birth. Look at the dangers you have been delivered from, the journeys you have been protected in, the seasonable help he has sent you, the suitable support He has afforded you in distress, the counsel He has given you in doubts, and the comforts He has provided you in sorrow and darkness. These are present with you in meditation. Every breath in your life is a gift of mercy. Do not forget the former favors bestowed on you and your family. An empty perfume bottle still smells when the perfume is gone. Then meditate upon your present mercies. How many do you enjoy—your house, family, body, and soul, are all full of blessings! Think of them particularly. Spread them out like jewels to your view. Meditate on how freely they are bestowed, on their fullness and greatness. But O, your soul's mercies—the image of God, the blood of Christ, eternal life, and seasons of grace! Your whole life is a bundle of mercies. These stir us up to bless the Giver. Then meditate on God to whom we pray. O how we are ashamed of our drops when we stand by the ocean! Meditate on His mercy and goodness.[2]

List or draw things for which you are grateful to God. Then echo this to Him.

Observe how this exercise, biblical thanksgiving, affects how you extend gratitude toward others. Without expressing thanks, your gratitude is incomplete. What changes are you beginning to see?

Holy Ground

- Spend an extended time in prayer with God.
  - ◉ Present to Him your struggles.
  - ◉ Echo your desire to "put on" and exhibit His character.
  - ◉ Ask for and lean into a greater dependence on His Holy

Spirit to manifest what is already true of you because you are in Christ. See Appendix 2b.

- God always does the initiating. Paul maintains that because of God's grace and Jesus's completed work on the cross, Christians are able to forgive. Spend an hour alone with God and let His Spirit bring to your attention someone in your life who needs forgiveness. You'll come up with all kinds of reasons not to do so, but let God have His way. It's called obedience. Record your thoughts from your time with God.

    Refer to the prayer found in Appendix 3. Allow God to show you how He sees this person because this is how He sees you. You may find it easier to forgive. How will you let God have His way?

- Describe your thoughts and emotions that arise when focusing on the mercies of God. How do these impact your soul?

- How does recognizing and acknowledging God's bountiful mercies extended to you impact the frequency of intentional expressions of gratitude to God? Your intentional expressions of gratitude to others? This intentionality can progressively become your nature.

One effective antidote to pride is the humbling posture of gratitude. It is the acknowledging that someone else did something for you that you did not expect, deserve, or could not or would not do for yourself. Thankfulness can strengthen your understanding of God's power. It helps us to know the difference between humbly accepting something granted to us and thoughtlessly taking it for granted.

‖‖‖‖‖‖‖‖‖‖‖‖‖‖‖‖‖‖‖‖‖‖‖‖‖‖‖‖‖‖‖

HISTORICAL SNAPSHOT

George Swinnock (c. 1627–1673) was a clergyman and ejected minister who was raised in the Maidstone, Kent, home of his uncle Robert Swinnock, a zealous Puritan and mayor of the town, following the early death of his father.

HEBREWS 12:1–3

Ground Rules

Twenty-one of the twenty-seven books of the New Testament are epistles or letters. If an apostle or another leader could not be physically present to address a church situation, the next best option was to write a letter and send it by personal courier. These written words carried the same authoritative weight as would the words spoken by the writer himself. Letters were occasional—not that these were randomly or sporadically written—but addressed a specific occasion or state of affairs. A behavior needing correcting (1 Corinthians 5:1–5, an incestuous man), a doctrinal error needing to be set right (Galatians 2:14, certain Jewish Christians [Judaizers] convincing Gentiles to observe Jewish religious customs, to "live like Jews"), or a misunderstanding (1 Thessalonians 4:16, confusion over "the dead in Christ").

A trained scribe or secretary (*amanuensis*) typically wrote a letter for the author. As there was no postal service, the finished copy would be hand delivered by a trusted individual, who could also answer questions to ensure a correct understanding of the letter. An epistle was meant to be read aloud again and again, not least because literacy was so low.

All of the epistles were written in the first century and follow the conventional format of a first century letter: the greeting, the body of the letter, and its conclusion. The greeting includes the name of the writer, name of the recipients, and an introductory opening prayer. Where this is missing, pay attention, because it means there is a serious matter about to be addressed. The body of a letter addresses the specific situation. And the letter ends with a closing grace benediction. Each epistle falls into one of two categories: Pauline, written by the apostle Paul and named after the recipients, and General or catholic, whose titles, except Hebrews, were the names of the non-Pauline authors.

As one would do today with an email or text message, read the whole of the letter in one sitting. This allows for the author's argument to be traced and better understood. You will find that the paragraphs make up the units of thought, not individual verses. Even as a whole, we still only understand half of the conversation, much like hearing one side of a phone conversation. This is where historical context comes in. Knowing what was going on when and with whom is most critical for reading and interpreting an epistle. Along with reading these letters historically, we can read them theologically, discovering what God reveals about Himself.

When reading any part of Scripture, the meaning of a passage is what the original author intended his audience to know and understand.

This is especially important when reading and interpreting the epistles because the epistle writer had a specific desired outcome for the reader(s) in response to his letter. Present-day implications and application should still be aligned with the author's intent.

Background

There are similarities in the letter to the Hebrews to Paul's writings, but not enough to confidently identify him or anyone else as its author. So, you'll typically hear the author referred to as "the writer of Hebrews." Whoever the author was, he served as a caring and committed Christian leader of a church. He was highly educated, knew the Old Testament, knew his audience and the circumstances they were facing, and knew how they were responding. Because of the extent of Old Testament knowledge the author assumes about his audience, the recipients appear to be Jewish Christians. Their faith in Christ was being tested and they were considering leaving the larger Christian community. Suffering and persecution seem to have compromised their desire and ability to persevere in the faith. Whatever the trial, they were likely to face it again.

The religion of the Jews was recognized by the Roman government. Christianity was not. One of the perks the Jews enjoyed was protection. Christians were targets. External persecution by state authorities was real, likely outweighed only by the internal, culture-imposed exclusion of those who followed Christ. A decision to follow Christ deeply severed family, friend, and business relationships. It meant the daily bearing of the shame and humiliation of living outside the convention of their cultural heritage. This posed the serious threat of falling away, leaving the faith, and leaving Jesus as Savior.

The writer of Hebrews wants his readers to be encouraged and to endure in their faithfulness to Christ. He reminds them that God has spoken most ultimately in the person and work of Jesus, who is God incarnate, and is superior to the prophets (Hebrews 1:1), mediating angels (Hebrews 1:5–14), Moses (Hebrews 3:1–19), Aaron (Hebrews 7:11), Levi's priesthood (Hebrews 7:1–25), Joshua (Hebrews 4:8), the whole priestly system (Hebrews 7:26–8:6), the Mosaic Covenant (Hebrews 8:7–13), the Tabernacle (9:1–7), Old Testament sacrifices (9:8–10:20), and any other proposed way of approaching God. Because Jesus is God's Son, and thus the faultless sacrifice, He is the perfect high priest (Hebrews 4:14–5:10; 7:1–28) who provides access to God for all. Quite an argument in this letter that reads like a sermon. Here is the warning: Rejecting Jesus means rejecting God.

Ground Work

- Pray a prayer of readiness and openness to God. Read Hebrews 11:1–12:3 twice through. Record any thoughts that come to mind.
- Looking for a hero? We all need one every once in a while. Someone, whether in person or on the pages of a book, whose life inspires, challenges, or assures us of a worthwhile outcome. Hebrews 11 is chock-full of them. Here you will find well-known and lesser known heroes who are described in a detailed synopsis or with an honorable mention. All are faith-marathoners, dispersed throughout the bright and dark ages of Israel's history.

  From the "Hall of Faith" in Hebrews 11, whose names are more familiar and whose are unfamiliar to you? Pick one of the lesser known characters, do a Bible search, jot a couple of facts here, and be encouraged.
- Reread the passage aloud. With the context in mind, record what might have been involved in the life of a new Hebrew believer in light of their decision to follow Jesus the Messiah.
- Read Hebrews 12:1–3. Urgently, the writer of Hebrews emboldens these wearied souls to ponder the antidote. Three times in these three verses, a form of the word "endured" is used. What does this reveal about Jesus?

> Ostracized for your faith. Belittled for your belief.
> Opinions ignored because you hold to the values of God and
>   His kingdom.
> Abilities overlooked because of whose you are.
> Bail. Jump ship. Cut your losses and move on.

Can you relate to any of the above? Soul fatigue. It is a condition not limited to the first century. Those believers experienced firsthand symptomatic soul fatigue. Persecuted and spent, many determined the price was too high. They were left with weak hearts and tired souls. Worn through and worn out, they had suffered enough contempt to consider abandoning the journey of faith. Are you tempted or do you know someone who is tempted by the green grass of giving in and giving up that looks more inviting with each glance?

- The third time "endured" is used occurs in the perfect tense (Hebrews 12:3). This Greek tense denotes a completed action whose effects are felt in the present, the time in which the writer pens this charge. There would be a present significance of Jesus's past enduring.

    How might your soul or the soul of a friend be encouraged by Jesus's tenacious endurance?

- What portion of this passage keeps drawing your attention? Record that portion. What attribute of God is brought to the forefront of your mind? What is your honest response? Take this to God in prayer.

Holy Ground

- Ponder. Think hard, the writer urges. Consider Him who endured such hostility from sinners. Think of Good Friday. Put yourself there and allow yourself to be captivated by it. Observe the backdrop God ordained. The self-centered political leaders were visiting from their distant homes. The hometown Jewish leaders, with their relentless efforts to eliminate this One who called God His Father and who established His Kingdom, were gathered in numbers for the kill. Sense the intensity of what was going on. His attackers targeted every part of Jesus's being: physical, mental, psychological, emotional, and spiritual. Only One remained steadfast to His calling and mission—Father-focused and others-centered—as He endured the ultimate in hate-motivated brutality. Jesus's endurance displays His committed love. Let the words of this passage sink into your soul. Consider the antidote for weary hearts and take hold of its intended soul-girding effect.

- Over the next few days, while commuting to work or running errands, turn off the radio or any device for music or news. Convert that time to time spent in conversation with God, reflecting on how Jesus "endured such hostility from sinners against Himself, so that you won't grow weary and give up." When able, jot your musings here.

- As God's Spirit guides, conference with a trusted friend to share that which has been resonating in your heart and soul. What new thoughts came to mind?

- Share the antidote of Jesus's humble enduring with someone who needs to hear and know such encouragement. Be a hero of a friend.

- Reread the passage. Spend some time alone reflecting on your recorded thoughts and the experience of sharing those thoughts. How has God spoken to you through His Word, His Spirit, and His community?

Appendix 1 (from Chapter 7)

The 1 Corinthians test is taken from 1 Corinthians 13:4–7.

Insert the name of a person at each blank. How did this person measure up against Jesus's standard?

_____ is patient, _____ is kind. _____ does not envy, _____ is not boastful, _____ is not arrogant, _____ is not rude, _____ is not self-seeking, _____ is not irritable, and _____ does not keep a record of wrongs. _____ finds no joy in unrighteousness but rejoices in the truth. _____ bears all things, believes all things, hopes all things, endures all things.

APPENDIX 2A (FROM CHAPTER 8)

Identity "in Christ" passages.

Complete the following sentence with a word or short phrase from your understanding of the verses found below.

Since I am IN CHRIST, by the Grace of God, I am

_____.

Romans 5:1—
Romans 6:1–6—
Romans 8:1—
1 Corinthians 1:30—
1 Corinthians 2:12—
1 Corinthians 2:16—
1 Corinthians 6:19, 20—
2 Corinthians 1:21—
2 Corinthians 5:14, 15—
2 Corinthians 5:21–22—
Galatians 2:20—
Ephesians 1:3—

Ephesians 1:4—
Ephesians 1:5—
Ephesians 1:7, 8—
Ephesians 1:13, 14—
Ephesians 2:5—
Ephesians 2:6—
Ephesians 2:18—
Ephesians 3:12—
Colossians 1:13—
Colossians 1:14—
Colossians 1:27—
Colossians 2:7—

Colossians 2:10—
Colossians 2:11—
Colossians 2:12, 13—
Colossians 2:14—
Colossians 3:1–4—
2 Timothy 1:7—
2 Timothy 1:9—
Titus 3:5—
Hebrews 2:11—
Hebrews 4:16—
2 Peter 1:4—

1. Before completing this worksheet, did you know who you are "in Christ"?

2. Make a list of the things that cause YOU to forget who you are "in Christ."

3. What does it look like when YOU forget who you are "in Christ"? What do YOUR relationships look like?

4. Spend at least a half an hour on what you have discovered and answered. Allow God to impress on your heart who you are "in Christ." How might knowing who you are in Christ impact a present situation? Be specific as you record your thoughts here.

Appendix 2B (from Chapter 8)

Since I am IN CHRIST, by the Grace of God, _____

Romans 5:1—I have been declared righteous and have peace with God.

Romans 6:1–6—I have died with Christ and died to the power of sin's rule over my life and now walk in newness of life.

Romans 8:1—I am free from condemnation.

1 Corinthians 1:30—I have been placed into Christ by God's doing.

1 Corinthians 2:12—I have received the Spirit of God into my life that I might know the things freely given to me by God.

1 Corinthians 2:16—I have been given the mind of Christ.

1 Corinthians 6:19, 20—I am a temple where God's Spirit dwells. I am not my own. I have been bought with a price. I belong to God and can glorify Him.

2 Corinthians 1:21, 22—I am strengthened, anointed, and sealed by God and given God's Spirit in my heart.

2 Corinthians 5:14, 15—I have died. I no longer live for myself, but for Jesus.

2 Corinthians 5:21—I have become the righteousness of God.

Galatians 2:20—The life I am now living is Christ's life.

Ephesians 1:3—I have been blessed with every spiritual blessing in the heavens.

Ephesians 1:4—I have been chosen in Christ before the foundation of the world to be holy and blameless in love before Him.

Ephesians 1:5—I was predestined (determined by God) to be adopted as His child.

Ephesians 1:7, 8—I have been redeemed, forgiven, and am a recipient of God's lavish grace.

Ephesians 1:13, 14—I have been sealed with the Holy Spirit, who is the pledge (deposit/down payment) guaranteeing my inheritance to come.

Ephesians 2:5—I have been made alive.

Ephesians 2:6—I have been raised up and seated with Christ in the heavens.

Ephesians 2:18—I have direct access to God through the Spirit.

Ephesians 3:12—I have boldness and confident access to God.

Colossians 1:13—I have been rescued from the domain of darkness (Satan's rule) and transferred into the kingdom of Christ.

Colossians 1:14—I have been redeemed and forgiven of all my sins.

Colossians 1:27—Christ Himself is in me.

Colossians 2:7—I have been firmly rooted in Christ and am now being built up in Him.

Colossians 2:10—I am filled (made complete) in Christ.

Colossians 2:11—I have been spiritually circumcised. My old, unregenerate nature has been removed.

Colossians 2:12, 13—I have been buried, raised, and made alive with Christ.

Colossians 2:14—The debt against me has been erased. It has been nailed to the cross.

Colossians 3:1–4—I have been raised up with Christ. I died with Christ; my life is now hidden with Christ in God. Christ is now my life.

2 Timothy 1:7—I have been given a spirit of power, love, and sound judgment.

2 Timothy 1:9—I have been saved and called according to God's own purpose and grace.

Titus 3:5—I have been saved. I am renewed by the Holy Spirit.

Hebrews 2:11—I am sanctified and am one with the Sanctifier (Christ), and He is not ashamed to call me His brother or sister.

Hebrews 4:16—I can come boldly before the throne of grace and receive mercy and grace to help me in time of need.

2 Peter 1:4—I have been given great and precious promises by God, so that I may share in the divine (God's) nature.

APPENDIX 3 (FROM CHAPTER 8)

A prayer taken from Psalm 139: 1–18, 23–24

Lord, You have searched _____ and known _____. You know when _____ sits down and when _____ stands up; You understand _____ thoughts from far away. You observe _____ travels and _____ rest; You are aware of all _____ ways. Before a word is on _____ tongue, You know all about it, LORD. You have encircled _____; You have placed Your hand on _____. This wondrous knowledge is beyond _____. It is lofty; _____ is unable to reach it.

Where can _____ go to escape Your Spirit? Where can _____ flee from Your presence? If _____ goes up to heaven, You are there; if _____ makes _____ bed in Sheol, You are there. If _____ lives at the eastern horizon or settles at the western limits, even there Your hand will lead _____; Your right hand will hold on to _____. If _____ says, "Surely the darkness will hide me, and the light around me will be night"—even the darkness is not dark to You. The night shines like the day; darkness and light are alike to You.

For it was You who created _____ inward parts; You knit _____ together in _____ mother's womb. _____ will praise You because _____ has been remarkably and wondrously made. Your works are wondrous, and _____ knows this very well. _____ bones were not hidden from You when _____ was made in secret, when _____ was formed in the depths of the earth. Your eyes saw _____ when _____ was formless; all _____ days were written in Your book and planned before a single one of them began.

God, how precious Your thoughts are for _____; how vast their

sum is! If _____ counted them, they would outnumber the grains of
sand; when _____ wakes up, _____ is still with You.

Search _____, God, and know _____ heart; test
_____ and know _____ concerns. See if there is any offensive
way in _____; lead _____ in the everlasting way.

Appendix 4 (from Chapter 11)

"One another" passages:

Leviticus 19:11—You must not steal, act deceptively, or lie to one another.

Leviticus 25:17—Do not cheat one another, but fear your God.

Jeremiah 7:5—Act justly to one another.

Zechariah 7:9—Show faithful love and compassion to one another.

Zechariah 8:16—Speak truth to one another.

Mark 9:50—Be at peace with one another.

John 13:34; 15:12, 17; Romans 13:8; 1 Peter 1:22; 1 John 3:11, 23; 4:7, 11; 2 John 1:5—Love one another.

Romans 12:10—Show affection to one another in brotherly love.

Romans 12:16—Live in harmony with one another. Do not be proud; instead associate with the humble. Do not be wise in your own estimation.

Romans 14:13—No longer judge one another. Decide never to put a stumbling block or pitfall in way of your brother or sister.

Romans 14:19—Pursue what promotes peace and builds up one another.

Romans 15:5—Live in harmony with one another.

Romans 15:7—Accept one another, just as Christ accepted you, to the glory of God.

Galatians 5:13—Because you are free, serve one another through love.

Galatians 5:26—Do not become conceited, provoking one another, envying one another.

Galatians 6:2—Carry one another's burdens.

Ephesians 4:2—With humility, gentleness, and patience, bear with one another in love.

Ephesians 4:25—Speak truth to one another.

Ephesians 4:32—Be kind and compassionate to one another, forgiving one another, as God forgave you in Christ.

Ephesians 5:19—Speak to one another in psalms, hymns, and spiritual songs.

Ephesians 5:21—Submit to one another.

Colossians 3:9—Do not lie to one another.

Colossians 3:13—Bear with one another and forgive one another, just as the Lord has forgiven you.

Colossians 3:16—Teach and admonish one another in all wisdom, singing psalms, hymns, and spiritual songs, with gratitude in your hearts to God.

1 Thessalonians 4:18, 5:11—Encourage one another.

1 Thessalonians 5:15—Pursue what is good for one another and for all.

Hebrews 10:24—Watch out for one another to provoke love and good works.

James 5:9—Do not complain about one another, so that you will not be judged.

James 5:16—Confess your sins to one another and pray for one another.

1 Peter 4:9—Be hospitable to one another without complaining.

APPENDIX 5: MEANS OF GRACE[1]

SILENCE AND SOLITUDE: The stillness of time and place where you are alert to the rumblings of the soul and the impressions of God, and where you find a deep willingness to stay and return.

FASTING: The response to God's prompting to intentionally deny the ever-pleasing me for a period of time from something (1) I know I need, (2) I have been convinced I need, or (3) I have been convinced I am entitled to have. We should fast for a period long enough to come to the point of recognizing the adhesive grasp something has over us and hearing our response to God's question, "Am I enough for you?"

PRAYER: Personally and deeply communicating and communing with God in words, thoughts, cries, or sighs. As we listen, we open ourselves to the divine impressions He places on the soul.

CONFESSION: When my soul agrees with what my heart knows to be true about my sin, no matter what the reason or cause, and without excuse. Genuine confession and repentance allow the soul to be most receptive to God's abundant, divine, life-transforming forgiveness.

BIBLICAL HOSPITALITY: The grateful response to God's extension of saving grace in indiscriminate acts of generosity and friendship toward strangers—fellow image bearers of God—while expecting nothing in return. Society's "unlovable" become the object of those whose hands, feet, voices, and presence embody Christ. Our hearts, like God's, beat for the last, least, and lost because of His desire that they be first, favored, and found.

BIBLICAL THANKSGIVING: The humble and responsive posture of the heart that expresses gratitude regardless of circumstances because it simply focuses on who God is and what He does. It starts with the internal recognition of our core needs and the acknowledgment of an all-knowing God and His loving-kindness—*hesed*. This is followed by an external expression of dependence on and adoration of God. We extend this thankfulness to those among us who are conscious or unconscious conduits of God's *hesed*. It is not found in a moment, a holiday, or a meal, but in a way of thinking and living wisely.

APPENDIX 6:
HISTORICAL SNAPSHOTS

JOSEPH ALLEINE (1634–1668) was an English dissenting minister and spiritual writer. He was ejected from his parish for failing to accept the Act of Uniformity and was indicted, fined, and then imprisoned for much of a year for preaching illegally. Despite ill heath, he continued to preach and was imprisoned again, defying two orders that limited preaching and gathering freedoms: the Conventicle Act and the Five Mile Act. His focus on the spiritual life is reflected in his *Christian Letters*, which contain exhortations to the congregation when they were separated by his imprisonment. Another work, *The Sure Guide to Heaven*, became a classic of Puritan devotion. He died at age thirty-four. See pages 144–45 and 147.

ISAAC AMBROSE (1604–1664) was a Church of England clergyman and author. He was briefly imprisoned on a few occasions and was ejected for Nonconformity in 1662. His writings are appreciated for their lively prose, eloquence, vividness, warmth, and urgency. His lengthy *Media* is a treatise on sanctification that addresses spiritual practices for a believer to grow in grace and intimate union with Christ. He is known for his commitment to systematic meditation and his annual month-long retreats. See pages 39 and 51.

RICHARD BAXTER (1615–1691) was an ejected minister and religious writer. Born into an impoverished family, he was impacted by the writings of Richard Sibbes, William Perkins, and Ezekiel Culverwell. He is well-known for his twenty-year ministry and spiritual investment in Kidderminster during the 1650s, commenting on its remarkable transformation: "When I came thither first, there was about one family in a street that worshipped God and called on his name," but "when I came away there were some streets where there was not past one family in the side of a street that did not so; on the Lord's Day . . . you might hear a hundred families singing psalms and repeating sermons, as you passed through the streets." Baxter was counted among two thousand preachers ejected from the clergy for refusing to subscribe to the Act of Uniformity. *The Reformed Pastor* was his contribution addressing pastoral neglect, but the gain from its wisdom for life is not limited to pastors. His published works number 135 with an additional six published posthumously. His best-known books are *The Saints Everlasting Rest, A Call to the Unconverted,* and *The Reformed Pastor.* See pages 38–39, 52, 83, 87, 103–4, 109, 112, 117–18, 120, 130–31, and 136.

NICHOLAS BOWND (died 1613) was a Church of England clergyman and religious writer, best known for his work *The Doctrine of the Sabbath.* He argues for the observance of rest, worship, and godly service on the Sabbath and for the cessation of matters that distracted from devotion and acts of mercy. The diversion of games and sports that profaned the day was criticized. With Richard Greenham as his stepfather and John Dod as his brother-in-law, Bownd traversed in godly circles. See pages 68 and 117.

JOHN BUNYAN (1628–1688) was one of the great figures of seventeenth-century Puritanism. His life began as the son of a poor tinker, and he himself became one. Though having a rudimentary education, he would eventually produce over sixty works. Though a powerful preacher, he was sent to prison for preaching without official rights from the king. His prison terms lasted for twelve years, during which he wrote a number of books, including his autobiography, *Grace Abounding to the Chief of Sinners* and *Pilgrim's Progress.* Second to the Bible, *Pilgrim's Progress* is the best-selling Christian book of all time. The characters in this master-piece are reflections of real people. During his incarceration, some jailers granted him occasional weekend releases to preach. He became ill on a journey to London and is buried in Bunhill Fields in London. See pages 13, 47, 57, and 73–74.

EDMUND CALAMY (1600–1666) was a clergyman, an ejected minister, and a popular and outspoken preacher. He was prominent in the English Civil War. Along with other Puritan leaders, Calamy accompanied Sir Robert Harley, who was married to Brilliana Harley (see Chapter 11) in presenting the "Ministers' petition and remonstrance" in 1641 with nearly a thousand signatures advocating reform of church government. Calamy was involved in the transformation of Sion College in London and became its president in 1650. Richard Baxter notes that Calamy was "much valued and followed by the London ministers, as their guide; and many frequently met at his house." His life reflected one committed to national reform. See page 38.

SAMUEL CLARKE (1599–1682) was a clergyman, an ejected minister, and a biographer. His tutor at Emmanuel College, Cambridge, was Thomas Hooker. He was twice president of Sion College but is most famous for the biographies of clerics and noble professors, producing testimonies of Puritans of worthy moderation and examples of life. One of his last acts as a minister was to perform the marriage of Richard Baxter to Margaret Charlton in 1662. His biography of his wife Katherine, in "A Looking Glass for Good Women to Dress Themselves by," included portions from her spiritual meditations. They were married nearly fifty years when she died at age seventy-three. See pages 73–74.

JOHN DOWNAME (1571–1652) was a Church of England clergyman, theologian, and author who came to prominence in the 1640s when he worked closely with the Westminster Assembly. He published treatises, biblical concordances, collections of sermons, and wrote ten books. Among the best known are *The Christian Warfare* and *A Guide to Godliness, or a Treatise of a Christian Life.* J. I. Packer writes, "Downame stands with Perkins, Greenham, and Richard Rogers as one of the architects of the Puritan theology of godliness." See pages 46 and 50.

WILLIAM GOUGE (1578–1653) was an English clergyman, author, and skilled expositor. His godly familial community included uncles Samuel and Ezekiel Culverwell and uncles through marriage William Whitaker and Laurence Chaderton. He preached three times each week, and after his Sunday morning sermons, those in the neighborhood who were poorer were invited to his home to discuss the sermon. His admirers called him "the father of the London Divines and the oracle of his time." A prolific writer, one of his most famous works, *Of Domesticall Duties*, provided an analysis of the godly household. See pages 83 and 110.

RICHARD GREENHAM (c. 1542–1594) was a Church of England clergyman and tireless preacher, known for his devotion to God, as evident through his life, ministry, and writings. He typically preached four times and catechized once each week, believing that teaching prepared the hearts of people for the preached sermon. As a physician of souls, he often dealt graciously with afflicted consciences and answered a variety of questions, having experienced the deep waters of painful conflicts himself. In an effort to equip those entering the ministry, Greenham established a rectory seminary. Some under his training, like Arthur Hildersham and Henry Smith, became well-known preachers and authors. See page 58.

BRILLIANA HARLEY (c. 1598–1643) was the daughter of the secretary of state, Sir Edward Conway. She was the third wife of the widower Sir Robert Harley and shared his Puritan views. The collection of approximately 375 letters sent to her husband and eldest son, Edward, offers clear evidence of domestic and maternal concerns in her married life, while also engaged in religious and political debates as a staunch Puritan and parliamentarian. Faced with the demands of the mid-seventeenth-century civil war, her actions depict the political and social role of elite English women. See pages 145–48.

MATTHEW HENRY (1662–1714) was a leading Nonconformist Puritan minister and distinguished devotional Bible commentator, known for his substantial *Commentary on the Whole Bible*. He was a frail child yet studious. Educated privately at home and primarily by his father, he was reading the Bible at three years of age. His study of God's Word continued throughout his life as a minister and he was known as a man of prayer. He began his commentary work at the age of forty-two. It was based on his system of expository preaching and the copious notes collected during his ministry. His ability to read, understand, and study God's Word was aided by his knowledge of Latin, Greek, and Hebrew languages learned as a child. See pages 53 and 72.

THOMAS HOOKER (1586–1647) was an English-born minister in America. Puritans Thomas Goodwin and Philip Nye pen this about Hooker: "If any of our late preachers and divines came in the spirit and power of John Baptist, this man did." Hooker's preaching delivered the truths of Scripture, but his messages against some Church of England rituals brought him to the anti-Puritan attention of Archbishop William Laud of Canterbury. Laud had Hooker ejected from his lectureship, or teaching post. Joining the Puritan exodus to America, Hooker set sail on an eight-week voyage to Massachusetts in 1633. He was a preacher, theologian, and prime mover in the creation of the colony of Massachusetts, who impacted both Englands. See pages 130–31.

WILLIAM LAUD (1573–1645) was appointed Archbishop of Canterbury in 1633. Laud reintroduced many Catholic forms of worship, supported Arminian theology, and prohibited the preaching of predestination. He required clerical dress and the use of the prayer book for all clergy and required laity to kneel while receiving communion. Laud unleashed a bitter persecution of Puritans, opposing the Puritan observance of the Sabbath by demanding that the *Book of Sports*, which was issued by James I in 1618 and reissued by Charles I in 1633, be read from every pulpit upon threat of suspension. The underhand and anti-Christian ways of the Laudian hierarchy caused many Puritans to emigrate to the Netherlands or New England. Laud was arrested and executed for treason on Tower Hill at the Tower of London in 1645. See page 68.

JONATHAN MITCHEL (1624–1668) was an English-born son of Puritan parents who migrated to Massachusetts when Mitchel was a young boy. A frail child, he suffered from a fever at age ten that disabled one of his arms for life. After graduating from Harvard College, he succeeded Thomas Shepard as pastor of the Cambridge congregation after Shepard's death. He is credited with coining the phrase *errand in the wilderness*, referring to New England's mission from God and was a leader in American Puritanism. His published work, "A Discourse of the Glory," enjoyed multiple editions. See pages 69, 143, and 147.

JOHN NORTON (1606–1663) was an English-born preacher who, because of the hostility of Archbishop Laud, immigrated to America. His work, *Abel being Dead Yet Speaketh*, is credited with being the first biography written in America and presents a short history of the life of John Cotton. It is with the impact that Cotton made and continued to make on others that Norton begins this work with these words, "It is the privilege of those who lived in heaven while they lived on earth that they may live on earth while they live in heaven." See page 84.

JOHN OWEN (1616–1683) was a theologian and minister who was called by some "the Calvin of England" and by others "the prince of the English divines." He entered Queen's College at the age of twelve, studying the classics, mathematics, philosophy, theology, Hebrew, and rabbinical writings. At age twenty-six, his forty-one-year writing career began and would yield more than eighty works. In writing on the spiritual life, this theological giant advocated renovating grace. He became dean of Christ Church College and later vice-chancellor of Oxford University. Influencing the lives of undergraduates, he required them to repeat Sunday sermons to "some person of known ability and piety." Owen is buried in Bunhill Fields in London along with many of his Puritan contemporaries. See pages 36 and 87.

WILLIAM PERKINS (1558–1602) indulged in recklessness, profanity, black magic, the occult, and drunkenness as a youth. While a student at Cambridge, he had a conversion experience that changed his personal life and led him to pursue theological studies. He excelled at Cambridge and in his early ministry preached to prisoners in the local jail. His close friends included Laurence Chaderton, Richard Greenham, Richard Rogers, and other Puritans. An accomplished theologian and author, Perkins's impact and influence was extended through other theologians, namely William Ames, Richard Sibbes, John Preston, and John Cotton. Perkins's *A garden of spirituall flowers* is one of the earliest Puritan devotional manuals. See page 84.

JOHN PRESTON (1587–1628) was a valued politician, influential teacher, powerful preacher, theologian, and renown author. Richard Sibbes and John Cotton mentored Preston, who in turn influenced others such as Thomas Goodwin and Thomas Shepard. His preaching became grounds to call him a "hotter sort of Protestant," and he was the leading Puritan of the 1620s. Preston's works focus on matters of spirituality and practical godliness as exemplified in his *Saints' Spirituall Strength*. He died a bachelor just short of his forty-first birthday. See pages 31, 37, and 39.

ROGER QUATERMAYNE was a seventeenth-century Puritan lawyer who was investigated by Archbishop Laud and others for the offense of holding religious meetings in circumstances that were politically as well as ecclesiastically suspect. Quatermayne records his experiences of arrest, inquisition, and imprisonment in *Quatermayns Conquest over Canterburies Court*, printed in 1642. Against the charge of holding an illegal conventicle, he states, "It is nothing but godly Conference, which every Christian man is bound to do and perform; for it is our duty to edify and build up one another in our most holy faith, which we cannot doe, except it be opened unto us." And his response to a warrant being served him, Quatermayne says there are "three things that made a man cheerful; a good God, a good Cause, and a good Conscience; and I praise God in this thing all these I have." See page 68.

JOHN ROGERS (c. 1570–1636) was not a model student at Emmanuel College, Cambridge. His uncle, Richard Rogers, provided for his education, but John was known to spend the money from the books he sold. After spending some time away, he returned to the university and to his old habits. When his uncle had nearly given up, his wife pleaded for one more opportunity. John Rogers completed his university studies with the third attempt. Rogers once impersonated God in a sermon, threatening to take away the Bible from an ungrateful people and then impersonated the people pleading for it to stay. Thomas Goodwin describes this message as having moved the audience to tears. Thomas Hooker sometimes called Rogers "The prince of all the preachers in England." Under the guise of a health caution, Archbishop William Laud suspended Rogers from preaching, only to find that after gaining health, his suspension continued. See page 68.

RICHARD ROGERS (1551–1618) was a Church of England clergyman and author. His set of "daily devotions" for godly life was expanded and became the work for which he is best known, *The Seven Treatises containing such directions as is gathered out of the Holy Scriptures*. This book shows how Christians can guide their lives by exercising various means of grace. His diary reveals details of his own personal devotions and his concern with manifesting living the godly life. It also reveals his frustration with the lack of Christian growth in godliness of those of his congregation. He enjoyed a strong friendship with fellow minister Ezekiel Culverwell. They discussed a variety of matters and received mutual encouragement from the time spent together in their life journeys. See pages 37, 129, 131, and 137.

TIMOTHY ROGERS (1658–1728) was a Nonconformist minister who suffered with clinical depression that lasted for nearly two years. A collection of Rogers' sermons on God's goodness in restoration to health became a work titled *Practical Discourses on Sickness and Recovery*. It was dedicated to two friends who provided a country stay for him during his "troubled and uneasy times." Among his several published funeral sermons, *The Character of a Good Woman, both in single and a married State* (1697) was preached for Elizabeth Dunton (1697), sister to Susannah Wesley, mother to Charles and John Wesley. See page 88.

FRANCIS ROUS (1579–1659) was a lay Puritan, religious writer, and politician. A deeply religious experience caused him to leave his legal studies to study theology. Rous's desire for reform of the English church that influenced his contributions to Parliament attested to his integration of theology and politics. Elected to Parliament in 1626, he served until his death in 1659. See page 122.

THOMAS SHEPARD (1605–1649) was a minister in both England and New England. Impacted by the preaching of John Preston, Shepard experienced a religious conversion that led him from disease and debauchery to his spiritual awakening and then to the ministry. Bishop William Laud silenced him and refused to allow him to minister in the district of London. After going into hiding, he eventually sailed to New England. Shepard was instrumental in founding Harvard College in 1636. His influence on religious thought impacted many, including Jonathan Edwards. See page 52.

RICHARD SIBBES (1577–1635) was one of the most influential Puritan divines, a celebrated pastor, preacher, and theologian. Sibbes was distinguished for a meek and quiet spirit. He was dedicated to providing biblical theology and making it relevant to the godly layperson. And though he never married, his circle of friendships included those with other ministers, teachers, and laypersons. His most popular work, *The Bruised Reed and Smoking Flax*, is a series based on Jesus's quoting of Isaiah in Matthew 12:20. See pages 45, 50–51, 55, 144, and 147.

HENRY SMITH (1550–1600) was commonly called the "Silver-tongued Preacher" and "the first preacher in the nation" by his contemporaries. He was from a wealthy and honorable family and studied under Richard Greenham, with whom he resided. Smith, like Greenham, was a moderate Puritan who sought reformation of individuals first and then the reformation of churches. Smith's *Works* is a collection of his sermons.

Of preaching, Smith would write, "To preach simply is not to preach unlearnedly, nor confusedly, but plainly and perspicaciously, that the simplest which do hear may understand what is taught, as if he did hear his name." See page 35.

EDMUND STAUNTON (1600–1671) was an ejected minister. Staunton's religious conversion is said to have followed a serious illness at about the age of eighteen and a narrow escape from drowning about 1620. He became known as "the searching preacher," who catechized the "younger and ignorant sort of people" and "taught them also from house to house." He was suspended for over three years for refusing to read the *Book of Sports*. After serving as head of Corpus Christi College, Oxford, he preached until he was silenced in 1662 and preached privately after that time. See page 74.

RICHARD STOCK (1569–1626) was a famed Puritan minister in London and an example to his people in conversation, charity, faith, and purity. His commentary on Malachi was published posthumously in 1641. It was brought out by his son-in-law, Samuel Torshell, and dedicated it to all Stock's "ancient Friends and Hearers." See page 57.

GEORGE SWINNOCK (c. 1627–1673) was raised in the Maidstone, Kent, home of his uncle Robert Swinnock, a zealous Puritan and mayor of the town, following the early death of his father. George Swinnock was a clergyman and ejected minister. His work, *The door of salvation opened*, contains a preface by Richard Baxter. Swinnock died at about the age of forty-six. See pages 187–88.

THOMAS TREGOSSE (c. 1670–71) was a Puritan minister who was silenced in 1662 by the Act of Uniformity and prohibited from preaching in a public place. He was arrested after it became known that his neighbors gathered to hear his preaching to his family. During his three-month stay in prison, he preached to fellow prisoners. Tregosse was remembered particularly for his gift of conference, pressing others to holiness through questions posed in conversations or by employing spiritual divertissement, turning unedifying conference to a more holy discourse. See page 119.

JOHN UDALL (c.1560–1592/3) was an author who also gained a reputation as an eloquent preacher with Puritan views. He has been called "one of the most fluent and learned of Puritan controversialists." Volumes of published sermons identified him with godly ideals. When he preached openly about the need for reform in the Church of England, the criticisms led to his being deprived of his pastorate. He was arrested and sentenced to death but eventually received a pardon from Archbishop Whitgift. A volume of expository sermons, *Obedience to the Gospell*, was specifically intended for "the congregation of Christ's people, embracing the truth of the Gospel." See page 51.

THOMAS WATSON (died 1686) was a Puritan writer and pastor in London, known for his effective preaching and public prayer. He was ejected from his pastorate when the Act of Uniformity was passed in 1662. He preached when given the opportunity, whether it be in barns, in homes, or in the woods. Watson was a prolific writer, focusing on the spiritual life, classical, Hebraic and patristic learning. *A Body of Practical Divinity*, published posthumously, was Watson's most acclaimed work. *All Things Good* is a study of Romans 8:28. He pens that "showers of affliction water the withering root of their grace and make it flourish more." Watson explains how to use the various means of grace in *Heaven Taken by Storm*, based on Matthew 11:12. See pages 31–32 and 45.

NEHEMIAH WALLINGTON (1598–1658), was a turner (or lathe worker) and diarist. It was his habit to rise in the early hours of the morning and write before private prayer in his closet and further public prayers with his household. His fondness for books resulted in a library of more than two hundred works, beginning with William Gouge's *Of Domestical Duties*, which he purchased soon after he married. A rare glimpse of life through the eyes of a typical London Puritan artisan has been preserved through than 2,600 pages of personal papers and works—memoirs, religious reflections, sermon notes, political reportage, letters, and a spiritual diary. See page 104.

SUSANNA WESLEY (1669–1742) had a family heritage that was strongly Puritan. At a young age, however, Wesley chose to separate from Nonconformist ranks and join the established Church of England. She is best known for her role as mother to her large family. Her established rules and expectations for her children exhibited the "caring but authoritative discipline" of child-rearing practices. Sons Charles and John were cofounders of the Methodist movement. See pages 87–88.

The following sources were used for these Historical Snapshots:

Beeke, Joel. *Meet the Puritans*. Grand Rapids, MI: Reformation Heritage Books, 2006.

Bremer, Francis J. and Tom Webster, eds. *Puritans and Puritanism in Europe and America*. Santa Barbara, CA: ABC-CLIO, Inc., 2006.

Brook, Benjamin. *The Lives of the Puritans, in 3 Volumes*. London: Printed for James Black, 1813.

Gale, Theophilus. *The Life and Death of Thomas Tregosse*. London: (s.n.), 1671.

Kapic, Kelly M., and Randall C. Gleason. *The Devoted Life: An Invitation to the Puritan Classics*. Downers Grove, IL: InterVarsity Press, 2004.

Oxford Dictionary of National Biography

Pastoor, Charles, and Galen K. Johnson. *Historical Dictionary of the Puritans*. Lanham, MD: Scarecrow Press, 2007.

Quatermayne, Roger. *Quatermayns Conquest over Canterburies Court*. London, Printed by Tho. Paine, 1642.

Seaver, Paul S. *Wallington's World: A Puritan Artisan in Seventeenth-Century London*. Stanford: Stanford University Press, 1985.

NOTES

Foreword

1. Richard F. Lovelace, *Dynamics of Spiritual Life: An Evangelical Theology of Renewal* (Downers Grove, IL: InterVarsity Press, 1979), 232.

Introduction

1. Dhruv Khullar, "How Social Isolation Is Killing Us," *New York Times*, December 22, 2016.
2. Stephen C. Levinson, "Timing in Turn-Taking and Its Implications for Processing Models of Language" in *Frontiers in Psychology* (June 2015), 1–17.
3. Connie de Vos, Francisco Torreira, Stephen C. Levinson, "Turn-Timing in Signed Conversations: Coordinating Stroke-to-Stroke Turn Boundaries" in *Frontiers in Psychology*, vol. 6, (March 2015): 1–13.
4. *Oxford English Dictionary*, http://www.oed.com/view/Entry/38737?redirectedFrom=confer#eid.
5. "Confer" in *A New English Dictionary on Historical Principles; founded mainly of the material collected by The Philosophical Society*, ed. James A.H. Murray, vol. 2 (Oxford: The Clarendon Press, 1893), 799.

Chapter 1: Our Viral Hunger for Sacred Community

1. Miller McPherson, and Lynn Smith-Lovin, "Social Isolation in America: Change in Core Discussion Networks over Two Decades," *American Sociological Review* 71, no. 3 (June 2006): 353–54.
2. McPherson and Smith-Lovin, 372.
3. Lynn Smith-Lovin and Miller McPherson, "You Are Who You

Know: A Network Perspective on Gender," in *Theory on Gender/ Feminism on Theory, Social Institutions and Social Change*, ed. Paula England (New York: A. de Gruyter, 1993), 223–51.

4. Dallas Willard, "The Reality of the Spiritual Life," *Christian Spirituality and Soul Care Lecture Series*, Talbot School of Theology, Biola University, La Mirada, Fall 2006.

Chapter 2: What the Means of Grace Mean

1. C. S. Lewis, "On Edmund Spenser" in *Studies in Medieval and Renaissance Literature* (Cambridge: University of Cambridge Press 1966), 121.

2. C. S. Lewis, *The Screwtape Letters* (Old Tappan: New Jersey, 1976), 58.

3. John Preston, *Saints' Spiritual Strength* (London, 1637), 113–14. Keep this in mind as quotes from these saints of the past, slightly modernized for greater readability, are included in each chapter.

4. John Preston, *Remaines of that Reverend and Learned Divine John Preston* (London: Printed by R[ichard] [and John Legate]), 112.

5. Thomas Watson, *All Things for Good*, first published in 1663 as 'A Divine Cordial' (Banner of Truth Trust, 2001), 101.

Chapter 3: The Word Heard, Read, and Remembered

1. Henry Smith, *The Works of Henry Smith: Including Sermons, Treatises, Prayers, and Poems with Life of the Author*, ed. Thomas Fuller (Edinburgh: J. Nichol, 1866), 494.

2. Richard Rogers, *Seven Treatises* (London: Printed by the assignes of Thomas Man, 1630), 379.

3. John Owen, *The true nature of a Gospel church and its government* (London: Printed for William Marshall, 1689), 86.

4. John Preston, *Riches of mercy to men in misery* (London: Printed by J.T., 1658), 303.

5. Richard Rogers, *Seven Treatises* (London: Printed by the assignes of Thomas Man, 1630), 298.

6. Edmund Calamy, *The Happinesse of Those Who Sleep in Jesus* (London: Printed by J.H. for Nathanael Webb, 1662), 28.

7. Edward Calamy, *The Godly Man's Ark* (London: Printed for John Hancock, 1672), 34.

8. Preston, *Riches of Mercy*, 303.

9. Isaac Ambrose, *Media: The Middle Things* (London: printed by T.R. and E.M., 1652), 341.

10. Greenham, *Workes*, 385.

11. Richard Baxter, *Reformed Pastor*, ed. William Brown (Edinburgh: Banner of Truth Trust, 1974), 196.

12. Baxter, *The Reformed Pastor*, 174.

13. My gratitude to Doug Huffman for providing this overview.

14. Christopher Wright, "The Missional Nature and Role of Theological Education," presented as a Talbot Faculty Forum paper, 2/28/17, 9.

15. Wright, 7.

16. Bruce R. Bickel, *Light and Heat: The Puritan View of the Pulpit and The Focus of the Gospel in Puritan Preaching* (Morgan, Penn.: Soli Deo Gloria Publications, 1999), 1.

17. "State of the Bible 2017: Top Findings," *Barna*, https://www.barna .com/research/state-bible-2017-top-findings/.

18. David Kinnaman, *State of Pastors Webcast*, 1/17.

Chapter 4: "A Kind of Paradise": When Souls Were Refreshed

1. Watson, *Heaven Taken by Storm*, 72–73.

2. John Downame, *The Christian Warfare* (London: Printed by William Standsby, 1634), 259.

3. Anonymous, *Addresse*, 27.

4. Bunyan, *The Pilgrim's Progress* (Peabody, MA.: Hendrickson Publishers, 2004), 126.

5. John Downame, *A Guide to Godlynesse* (London: By Felix Kingstone and William Stansby, 1622), 76.

6. Richard Sibbes, *Bowels Opened* (London: Printed by R. Cotes, 1648), 298–299.

7. Sibbes, *Bowels Opened*, 296.

8. Isaac Ambrose, *Media: The Middle Things* (London: Printed by T. R. And E. M., 1652), 339.

9. Ambrose, *Media*, 341.

10. John Udall, *Obedience to the Gospell* (London: Imprinted [by J. Windet?], 1584), no pagination.

11. Baxter, *Reformed Pastor*, 196.

Chapter 5: Peek to Pique: Features of Conference

1. Bruce Demarest, *Satisfy Your Soul*, and personal communique with Dallas Willard.

2. Nicholas Bownd, *Sabbathum Veteris et Noui Testamenti: or the true doctrine of the Sabbath* (London: By Felix Kyngston, 1606), 402.

3. Sherry Turkle, *Reclaiming Conversation: The Power of Talk in a Digital Age* (New York: Penguin Press, 2015), 36.

4. Richard Sibbes, *Bowels Opened* (London: Printed by R. Cotes, 1648), 295.

5. Richard Stock, *A learned and very usefull commentary upon the whole prophesie of Malachy* (London: Printed by T.H. and R.H. for Thomas Nichols, 1641), 261.

6. Richard Greenham, *Workes* (London: Imprinted by Felix Kingston, for Cuthbert Burbie, 1605), 228.

7. Sherry Turkle, *Reclaiming Conversation*, 10.

8. Mark Zuckerberg, Facebook posting, January 18, 2017.

Chapter 6: Small (and Deeper) Group Conferences

1. Anonymous, *Stated Christian Conference asserted to be a Christian duty* (London: Printed for, and sold by Will. Marshal, 1697), 23.

2. R.J. Acheson, *Radical Puritans in England 1550–1660* (London: Routledge, 2013), 31.

3. R.J. Acheson, *Radical Puritans*, 30.

4. Nicholas Bownd, *Sabbathum Veteris Et Noui Testamenti: Or the True Doctrine of the Sabbath* (London: By Felix Kyngston, 1606), 391.

5. John Rogers, *A Treatise of Love* (London: Printed by H. Lownes and R. Young, 1629), 149–50.

6. Jonathan Mitchel, *A discourse of the glory* (London: Printed for Nathaniel Ponder, 1677), 15.

7. Ed Stetzer and Eric Geiger, *Transformational Groups: Creating a New Scorecard for Groups* (Nashville: B&H Books, 2014), 8.

8. Ed Stetzer and Eric Geiger, *Transformational Groups*, 10.

9. Robert Wuthnow, *Sharing the Journey* (New York: The Free Press, 1994), 19.

10. Gallup and Lindsay, *The Gallup Guide: Reality Check for 21st Century Churches* (Group Publishers, 2002), 14.

11. Todd Heatherton and Patricia Nichols, "Personal accounts of successful versus failed attempts at life change," *Personality and Social Psychology Bulletin*, vol. 20 no. 6 (1994): 669.

12. I thank Dr. Arianna Molloy Yeh for her direction in this area. She builds her approach to roles from Gloria J. Galanes and Katherine L. Adams, *Effective Group Discussions: Theory and Practice* (New York: McGraw-Hill, 2014).

13. Matthew Henry, "Proverbs" in *Matthew Henry's Commentary on the Whole Bible*, Vol. 3 (Peabody, MA.: Hendrickson, 1991), 743.

14. Richard Younge, *A touch-stone to try (by our knowledge, belief, and life) whether we be Christians in name only, or Christians in deed* (London: and are to be sold by Andrew Crooke, 1648), 6–7.

15. Samuel Clarke, *The lives of sundry eminent persons* (London: Printed for Thomas Simmons, 1683), 4.

16. John Bunyan, *Grace Abounding to the Chief of Sinners* (London: Printed by George Larkin, 1666), 11.

17. John Bunyan, *The Pilgrim's Progress* (Peabody, MA.: Hendrickson Publishers, 2004), 72.

18. Amit Sood, *The Mayo Clinic Guide to Stress-Free Living* (Boston, MA: Da Capo Lifelong Books, 2013), 239.

19. Summarized findings from Stetzer and Geiger, *Transformational Groups*, 41–46.

Chapter 7: Family Conferences of the Conversation Kind

1. William Gouge, *Workes* (London: Printed by John Beale, 1627), 10.

2. William Perkins, *A Garden of Spirituall Flowers* (London: Printed by R. B[adger], 1638), 119.

3. J. I. Packer, "The Puritans and the Lord's Day" in *Puritan Papers*, Vol 1, ed. J. I. Packer (Phillipsburg, NJ.: P&R Publishing, 2000), 98.

4. John Norton, *Abel being dead yet speaketh* (London: printed by Tho. Newcomb for Lodowick Lloyd, 1658), 6–7.

5. Robert Saucy, *Minding the Heart: The Way of Spiritual Transformation* (Grand Rapids: Kregel Publications, 2013), 212.

6. Bruce Waltke, *The Book of Proverbs: Chapters 1–15*, NICOT (Grand Rapids: Eerdmans, 2004), 1:295.

7. Timothy Rogers, *The Character of a Good Woman* (London: Printed for J. Harris, 1697), 48–49.

8. Charles Wallace, *Susanna Wesley: The Complete Writings* (Oxford: Oxford Univ. Press, 1997), 373.

9. "Top Ten Findings on Teens and the Bible," *Barna*, www.barna.com /research/top-10-findings-teens-bible/

10. The American Freshman: National Norms, Fall 2016, *Higher Education Research Institute*, www.heri.ucla.edu

11. Sherry Turkle, *Reclaiming Conversation*, 16–17, 21.

Chapter 8: Marriage Conferences
of the Conversation Kind

1. Baxter, *Godly Home*, 143.

2. British Library, Add. MS. 40,883, fo.176V.

3. Nehemiah Wallington, Folger MS. V.a.436, which is given the running title of "An Extract of the Passages of My Life and A Collection of Several of My Written Treatises," 1654. Folger MS V.a.436, 432.

4. William Gouge, *Building a Godly Home: A Holy Vision for a Happy Marriage*, vol. 2, edited and modernized by Scott Brown and Joel R. Beeke (Grand Rapids: Reformation Heritage Books, 2013), 70.

5. These statements are sponsored by the Center for Marriage and Families at the Institute for American Values and the National Marriage Project at the University of Virginia. Sponsored by the

Center for Marriage and Families, chaired by W. Bradford Wilcox of the University of Virginia.

6. Gary Thomas, *Sacred Marriage* (Grand Rapids: Zondervan, 2000), 13.

7. Tim Muehlhoff, *I Beg to Differ* (Downers Grove: InterVarsity Press, 2014), 36.

8. Robert Saucy, *Minding the Heart* (Grand Rapids: Kregel Publications, 2013), 220.

9. Barbara Myerhoff, "Life History Among the Elderly: Performance, Visibility, and Re-Membering," *A Crack in the Mirror: Reflexive Perspectives in Anthropology*, ed. Jay Ruby. (Philadelphia: University of Pennsylvania Press, 1982), 103.

10. Richard Baxter, *The Godly Home*, ed. Randall J. Pederson (Wheaton, Ill.: Crossway, 2010), 141–42.

11. William Gouge, *Building a Godly Home*, 71.

12. Tony Reinke, *12 Ways Your Phone Is Changing You* (Wheaton, Ill.: Crossway, 2017), 43.

13. John Gottman and Nan Silver, *The 7 Principles for Making Marriage Work* (New York: Harmony Books, 2015), 60, 62.

14. Tim Muehlhoff, *I Beg to Differ*, 95–99.

15. Baxter, *Godly Home*, 141.

Chapter 9: From Pastor to Pew and Back Again

1. Nicholas Bownd, *The Doctrine of the Sabbath* (London: Printed by the Widdow Orwin, 1595), 220.

2. Charles Lloyd Cohen, *God's Caress: The Psychology of Puritan Religious Experience* (New York: Oxford Univ. Press, 1986), 163.

3. Baxter, *The Reformed Pastor*, 94–95.

4. Richard Baxter, *The poor man's family book* (London: Printed by R.W. for Nevill Simmons, 1674), 1.

5. Richard Rogers, *Seven Treatises* (London: Imprinted by Felix Kyngston, 1616), 32.

6. Samuel Clarke, *The lives of sundry eminent persons* (London: Printed for Thomas Simmons, 1683), 122.

7. Baxter, *The Reformed Pastor*, 178.

8. John R. W. Stott, *Between Two Worlds: The Art of Preaching in the Twentieth Century,* first American ed. (Grand Rapids: W. B. Eerdmans, 1982), 192.

9. Francis Rous, "The Mystical Marriage" (London: Printed by William Iones, dwelling in Red-crosse-streete, 1631), 113.

10. Ray Anderson, *The Soul of Ministry: Forming Leaders for God's People* (Louisville, KY.: Westminster John Knox Press,1997), 219.

Chapter 10: Not Your Typical Pastors Conference

1. Tom Webster, *Godly Clergy in Early Stuart England: The Caroline Puritan Movement c.1620–1643* (Cambridge: Cambridge University Press, 1997), 59.

2. Richard Baxter, *The Reformed Pastor,* ed. William Brown (Edinburgh: Banner of Truth, 1974), 71.

3. Cotton Mather, *Magnalia Christi Americana: Or, the Ecclesiastical History of New-England from its First Planting in the Year 1620 Unto the Year of Our Lord 1698,* Book III, Research Library of Colonial Americana (New York: Arno Press, 1972), 59–60.

4. John Fuller, "To the Reader," introduction to *The Journal or Diary of a Thankful Christian,* by John Beadle (London: Printed by E. Cotes, 1656), n.p.

5. John Fuller, *The journal or diary of a thankful Christian* (London, Printed by E. Cotes, 1656), n.p.

6. Richard Baxter, *Reliquiae Baxterianae* (London: Printed for T. Parkhurst, 1696), 13.

7. Rogers and Ward, *Two Elizabethan Puritan Diaries,* 53.

8. Barna Research, *The State of Pastors* (Ventura: Barna Group, 2017), 42.

9. C. S. Lewis, "The Barrier Breached," in Sheldon Vanauken, *A Severe Mercy* (New York: Harper & Row, Publishers, 1980), 134.

10. Richard Rogers, *Two Elizabethan Puritan Diaries,* ed. M. M. Knappen (Chicago: The American Society of Church History, 1933), 67.

11. Rogers, *Two Elizabethan Puritan Diaries,* 99.

12. Rogers, *Two Elizabethan Puritan Diaries*, 64.

13. Rogers, *Two Elizabethan Puritan Diaries*, 5.

14. Burns, *Resilient Ministry: What Pastors Told Us About Surviving and Thriving* (Downers Grove, IVP Books, 2013), 33.

15. Peter Scazzero, *Emotionally Healthy Spirituality* (Grand Rapids: Zondervan, 2014), 32.

16. John Brown, *Puritan Preaching in England: A Study of Past and Present* (New York: Charles Scribner's Sons, 1900), 140–141.

Chapter 11: Distance Conferencing

1. This chapter is written with awareness of the growing infusion of technology in our lives and concern for the accompanying addiction, dependency, distraction, and resulting loneliness and isolation. It is the author's hope and intent to redeem a practical and meaningful use of technology for the purposes of spiritual growth.

2. Jonathan Mitchel, *A Discourse of the Glory* (London: Printed for Nathaniel Ponder, 1677), 1–2.

3. Richard Sibbes, "A consolatory letter to an afflicted conscience" (London: Printed for Francis Coules, 1641), 1.

4. Ibid., 6.

5. Joseph Alleine, *Christian Letters full of spiritual instructions tending to the promoting of the power of godliness, both in person and families* (London; Printed for and sold by Nevil Simmons and Dorman Newman, 1673), 71.

6. Alleine, *Christian letters*, 73.

7. Brilliana Harley, *Letters of the Lady Brilliana Harley, Wife of Sir Robert Harley, of Brampton Bryan, Knight of the Bath: With Introduction and Notes by Thomas Taylor Lewis*, vol. LVIII (London: Printed for the Camden Soc., 1854), 65.

8. Harley, *Letters*, 139.

9. Earlier adopters to this newer frontier of distance conferencing are highlighted for their promising efforts as they advance toward more regularly and intentionally incorporating biblical truths into conversations through digital means.

10. Richard Sibbes, *A Consolatory Letter to an Afflicted Conscience* (London: Printed for Francis Coules, 1641), 1.

11. Gary McIntosh, "How are People Actually coming to Faith Today?" *Biola Magazine* (Fall 2016), 14.

Part III: Soul-to-Soul Bible Studies: Conferencing through God's Word

1. It is conceivable that Lydia (Acts 16:14, 15, and 40), is "the woman from Lydia of Asia Minor" and whose formal name is either Euodia or Syntyche.

2. The meditation is taken from Voices from the Past, a Puritan devotional by Richard Rushing, vol. 1, devotional for 11/11, page 316. It is an updated compilation of Swinnock's words from The Christian-man's calling (London: Printed by J.B. for Thomas Parkhurst, 1662), 100–102.

Appendix 5

1. Further descriptions of these and other means of grace can be found in Joanne J. Jung, *Knowing Grace: Cultivating a Lifestyle of Godliness* (Downers Grove, IL: InterVarsity Press, 2011).